India

A Cultural Decline or Revival?

India

A Cultural Decline or Revival?

Bharat Gupt

D.K. Printworld (P) Ltd.
New Delhi

Cataloging in Publication Data — DK
[Courtesy: D.K. Agencies (P) Ltd. <docinfo@dkagencies.com>]

Gupt, Bharat, 1946-
India : a cultural decline or revival? / Bharat Gupt.
p. cm.
ISBN 13: 9788124604595
ISBN 10: 8124604592

1. India — Civilization. 2. India — Social conditions.
3. Caste — Political aspects — India. I. Title.

DDC 954 22

ISBN 13: 978-81-246-0459-5 (HB) ISBN 10: 81-246-0459-2
ISBN 13: 978-81-246-0460-1 (PB) ISBN 10: 81-246-0460-6

First Published in India in 2008

Published and printed by:
D. K. Printworld (P) Ltd.
Regd. office : '*Sri Kunj*', F-52, Bali Nagar
New Delhi - 110 015
Phones : (011) 2545 3975; 2546 6019; *Fax* : (011) 2546 5926
E-mail: dkprintworld@vsnl.net
Web: www.dkprintworld.com

Dedicated to

Abhinav, Harleen

and

Udayan

Preface

It is often taken for granted in India that political Independence from British rule also ushered an era of cultural and social freedom. It is further imagined that in spite of its poverty, India is admired by the richer nations of the West as a culturally evolved nation. This self-congratulation, lingering from the euphoric days of our freedom struggle, sounds now like the thunder on distant mountains shedding not a glimmer of hope on our present lives.

For most of us our memory is enough to be a lived-through account of the cultural decline that set in barely within a decade after freedom. Any analysis is sufficient to counter the smug belief, still fostered in schools and political speeches about the superiority of our culture, once voiced in Iqbal's song, "*Saare jahaan se acchaa hindostaan hamaaraa*". Very insidiously this rhyme nurses a misplaced conviction that while many other ancient civilizations were wiped out in time, India alone is indestructable (*Yunaan-o-Misr-o-Romaa sab mit gaye jahaan se/ Ab tak magar hai baaqi naam-o-nishaan hamaaraa!/ Kuchh baat hai ki hastee mitatee naheen hamaaree/ Sadiyon rahaa hai dushman daur-i-zamaan hamaaraa*). Greek, Egyptian and Roman civilizations were wiped out from the earth/ But we alone have survived and kept our name and fame/ There is something that keeps our identity from elimination/Although we have had enemies for centuries together). The song takes special pride in stating that while the Greek and Roman civilizations, the so-called predecessors of the West, lost to ravages of time, Indian civilization alone remains immortal. Such headiness was excusable during the struggle for freedom but is hardly justified after half a century of self-misrule. Our name and significance (*naam-o-nishaan*) are now under gradual but marked erosion, fading faster than anything witnessed in the last millennium. The ravages of technology are greater than even those perpetrated by the Islamic misrule. In every sphere of life it is now obvious that India has not been able to internalize European technology to match its own civilization concepts, the foreign techno-*kaayaa* into its traditional *dharma-kaayaa*.

After Independence, each passing decade, except the first, ushered in an uncomfortable and dislocating change. In spite of the great violence experienced during the territorial reordering at Independence, only the decade of fifties was characterized by hope, within India, and as well in the minds of her well wishers. She was expected to perform by leaps as a developing nation by the international community. The optimism of this decade was symbolized by India's first Prime Minister, called "Chaachaa Nehru" by his sychophants who spent his every birth day, November 14th, with school-children as a state ritual. He projected the expectation that the nation was going to grow big and strong like its children. Every year, in the capital of the re-born nation, international exhibitions connected its people to the big and small nations of the world. Perhaps in the fifties only the country like its kids and their *Chaachaa* could smile hopefully.

In the sixties, things continued to take some shape as schools and colleges expanded. New factories and dams, Nehru's "temples of modern India", gave employment to many. Yet the less lucky but more enterprising started moving to far off lands in larger numbers. The present prosperous lot of the Indian diaspora in North America and Europe left the country at this time. By now the stagnation in the economic growth of Socialist order that an unchallenged Nehru had foisted upon the newly born sovereign nation began to extract its wages. Nevertheless, because of a strong nationalism, in spite of a heavy bullying by China (1962) and a severe injury by Pakistan (1965), India was able to defend most of its territory and reaffirm its identity.

The seventies, in their first half, witnessed another triumph of nationalism when Indira Gandhi played midwife to the birth of Bangladesh terminating a horrendous genocide of the Bangla Muslims and Hindus by the Punjabi Muslim army of West Pakistan. But giddy from her success she unheedingly consolidated the Socialist agenda to prune it of all liberal intellectual and democratic vitality that Nehru would have not have liked to disappear. While Indira Gandhi imagined herself much taller than actual, the turning point in the history ushered itself imperceptibly. By the mid-seventies darker days set in. External support to terrorism and internal regional factionalism cast their net around the nation. Both were promoted under many garbs by a pernicious propaganda masterminded in the bastions of Western subversive agencies and academics as well.

To contain the politically centrifugal forces, Indira Gandhi, flushed with her earlier success, made the pendulum of State governance swing from the dictatorial Socialism at the center to conspiratorial manipulations in the regions, thus seriously eroding democracy. This period was also beset with a grand illusion shared by all at the Left of center. They imagined that socialism could be poured from the top and changes at the grassroots would follow. The consequences of this make-belief were disastrous. Socialism created a class of corrupt politicians who acquired total control over national wealth and perpetuated a permit-raj that killed personal enterprise and initiative, while very little from the State percolated to the poor. On the cultural front, in the name of secularism, religious regression was promoted not only among minorities, but more so in the Hindu majority. Under the policy of nurturing parochial minions for Centrist manipulations, regional outfits were promoted to the extent that they went out of hand. By the end of the decade both the Socialist state and nationalism came to be discredited.

No wonder that the eighties were a decade of the first terrorist wars, caste polarization and withering of Socialist State that revealed the monumental corruption operating beneath. It is now established that in the early eighties, while a proxy war was begun against us by Pakistan in Punjab and Kashmir, another section of Indian policy-makers particularly from Tamil Nadu, sympathized with the terrorist and separatist outfit of Liberation Tigers of Tamil Elam including training terrorists and supplying arms from the mainland. It is already clear that instead of providing diplomatic, political and moral support to Sri Lankan Tamils suffering at the hands of Singhalese fanaticism, some sections of Indian authorities and the Tamil people chose the path of fuelling militancy, a strategy of intervention of which the nation itself was and still is a victim at the hands of others. But the final blunder of sending the Indian Peace Keeping Force to eliminate LTTE was beyond belief and dealt a severe blow to nationalism.

Nationalism suffered not only at the hands of separatist movements, but also even more through internal struggles along caste lines that further weakened its social suppleness for absorbing technology and ushering modernity while keeping its heritage. The ensuing caste strife diverted India from playing its important role in leading the colored and the colonized nations of the world in the international arena. The consolidation of the middle castes, which had acquired enough economic muscle to translate their cultural identity into a political clout, was subverted by ideologues like VP Singh, working consciously or unconsciously, under the impact of Western notions of ethnicity and compensatory discrimination under the garb of affirmative action for the so called Other Backward Classes. The results were counter productive and hyper-regressive that set the clock backwards and impeded the much needed technological advances. Like all upwardly mobile castes in the history of India, the Other Backward Classes (OBC) have mostly re-enforced the regressive values upheld by the upper caste elite. Even at the present juncture, their messiahs of reform are desperately re-inventing the economics of a decrepit Socialism and the non-democratic hierarchy of the *varna-jaati* system. Their slogan of 'social justice' has become another name for social stagnation riding rough on the backs of the lowest castes. Reiteration of the caste identities has not only subverted Indian nationalism, it has also made international open mindedness impossible at the grass-root level.

At the end of nineties, there was a continuation of proxy wars, a greater erosion of national unity, a tighter grip of casteism, and the ping-pong battle between the die-hards of the command economy and the uninformed votaries of liberalization. While in the West, liberalization, in spite of the evils of a rapid transition, is seen as the unquestioned option after the shattered Socialism, in India on the contrary, half way into the first decade of the 21st century, the Socialist Juggernaut has too many high priests and acolytes to let the *yaatraa* be called off. These priests, spear headed by the Marxist parties, have promptly substituted the doctrine of class struggle with that of caste struggle (in India, class is caste, they say) and pinned their hopes on affirmative action for social justice to keep their Juggernaut rolling. So far, "social justice" has only promoted a "*rabree* layer" (cream of the caste) that has virtually stalled the liberalization of the economy and more so of thought. Not only the Leftists, but even the rightists like the BJP (Bharatiya Janata Party), are not in favour of democratic privatization as that shall inevitably lead to the end of permit raj and may impel their vote bank of the middle level businessmen to find new loyalties. In India, even products of Harvard Business School talk Internet but practice Inspector-net by demanding tax returns from persons using minor essential amenities like a telephone or a car.

Every political party, for a handful of votes or a momentary alliance, pampers the regional, religious, or caste identities. For instance, the BJP may find in DMK (Dravida Munetra Kadgam) an attractive partner forgetting its decades of anti-Hindi-Sanskrit venom, or to pamper Sikh obscurantists, it can exempt helmets for Sikh women riding two-wheelers, or to protect its trader-tenant voters it can reverse a new rent bill, or declare the Jats as a backward caste as in Rajasthan for a few votes. It can adopt the same tactics of "pseudo secularism" for garnering popular support perfected by the Congress, equally mindless of the fragmentation these tactics generate. It aims at enlarging its base by relying on the same brahmin-bania-obc-minority combine with which the Congress made its salad-bowl for decades. The bowl was toppled for some time by Mandalism, but the basket of permit-raj with the vegetables of "ethnic plurality" and "minority rights" remain as of old, to be arranged by this or that hand.

The new millennium has opened with a glaring entropy in the Indian political system and social institutions. The ruling elite of legislators and bureaucrats is unable to handle even every day governance let alone crisis situations that are routine as sunrise. National interest seems to have been totally sacrificed at the altar of power struggle and corruption. In such a scenario there is a temptation to throw cultural matters in the background and focus on enforcement of law and defense of national territory. But this is not an age of territorial invasions. It is the age of cultural invasion and subversion. Political territories are altered after the cultural landscape has been reordered from within. Formation of new nations out of Yugoslavia is the most recent example. India has to resist that fate as the same strategies are being used against her. Most unfortunately her ruling classes are abetting the break up. There are three distinct forces that have at present laid a strong siege of India after the Cold War and the fall of her politically supportive though hardly economically beneficial ally, namely the Soviet Union. They are,

Commerial Globalism, Jehadi Islam and Evengelical Christianity. India needs a new leadership to counter these three. This requires strategies born of a cool and analytical mind and least of all an emotional retaliation of the momentary kind that seems to be the fashion of the day.

The *Mahabharata* contains a *shloka* that has found its way into many later day classical texts. Presumably, it offers a *neeti* or practical ethics for organizing a humane social order that provides as much for the single person as for its larger units.

> *Tyajedekam kulasyaarthe graamaarthe kulam tyajet, Graamam tyajet janapadasyaarthe aatmaarthe prithveem tyajet.*
>
> Give up the individual for the family, the family for the habitat, the habitat for land. But for the Aatman, give up the whole earth.

The *Eka, Kula, Graama, Janapada, Prithvee* and *Aatman* make up the mental and terrestrial shells for the inner and outer being of an individual in Indian terms. The changes that have taken place in these areas can index the decline or revival in cultural life.

Eka is the individual, male or female, that makes up the unit of cultural consciousness and the fulcrum of creative ability. If the *Eka* breaks either due to a hostile social environment or due to lack of inner ethical strength, the social order that depends upon individuals will also collapse. But so it shall also if the individual is unable to give up one's selfish interest for the larger unit of *Kula* (family), the family for *Graama* (habitat), the *Graama* for *Janapada* (regional kingdom/political unit/nation), and the *Janapada* for *Prithvee* (earth) and all material interests of the earth for the *Aatman* (Self). The mode of this non selfish action varies with time and place but as a principle for action it is none other than what Socrates called the Supreme Good (*ton agathon*) and what the Indian philosophers have called *dharma.*

The state of cultural excellence in a country cannot be measured in terms of its economic prosperity or the number of books in her libraries or the volume of her performers and professors that tour abroad. It is seen in her ability to lead a life that creatively satiates her worldly and transcendental desires and her ability to defend and preserve the institutions that train her people to lead such a life.

The present book is divided into six sections: *Eka*, *Kula*, *Graama*, *Janapada*, *Prithvee* and *Aatman*. I have chosen these terms as they not only define the Indian cultural experience more accurately than the Western categories like the 'individual', 'society', 'nation' and the 'global order'. The ancient *Janapada* was neither synonymous with the modern nation state or *raashtra*, nor with the present day provinces of a nation state. It was a local cultural space with community governance that enforced a moral and financial discipline that mattered much more for a person than the distant court of an emperor or the defacto emperor. In the age of nationalism and globalization, it has been virtually replaced for the time being by the nation state and will be further replaced by a newer entity.

But beneath the present 'regional states' and the nation state of India, the *Janapada* is still alive as a cultural force that seriously affects the behaviour of the rural Indian. It offers him a sustenance through festivals, dress and cuisine, colour and designs that are more rewarding than the 'week-end' is to the metro-Indian. The six categories seem more natural not only to understand the Indian identity of the past, but also to develop a healthier framework for personal, social and cosmic organization for the future. More than anything else, as indicated in the verse from the *Mahabharata*, they provide a well tested way (*marga / pantha*) to progress from the personal to the universal.

I am grateful to my friend, Sh. Ramesh Bindra for repeatedly proof-reading the text of this book. Several other friends and scholars who made suggestions and corrections are also to be thanked.

May 8, 2008 Bharat Gupt

Contents

Part One

EKA : The Uprooted Individual

1

The Ritual Universe

In the fifties, modernity came to be concretized in India as print culture managed space in which the symbolic and imaginative were replaced by functional reality. Although there had been many attacks on hypocrisy in Hindu rituals, a century earlier, by Dayanand Saraswati, Vivekanand, Phule, Sri Aurobindo and many other enlightened souls of modern India, the essential efficacy of a ritual was not denied by these reformers. It is important to note in the context of rituality that Dayanand Saraswati in spite of his virulent attack on *moorti* worship, reinvented and revived the Vedic *yajna* ritual and made it accessible in a very simple form to the traditionally uninitiated but a self chosen *arya-samaajee* worshiper. Vivekanand also advocated for the clean traditions of *saguna* worship.

But a great change of attitude towards the very value of ritual set in after Independence. In the state-manipulated intellectual climate that prevailed during Nehru's rule, reality and truth came to be defined in realistic Newtonian terms of European physical sciences. Rationality was reduced to a scientific positivism which was hyped as 'scientific temperament' and was privileged as a curative for the earlier 'non scientific Hindu vision' of the universe. What is worse, this fascination for 'scientific temperament' did not take into account the post-classical developments in physics and their implications on philosophy. Not only were some of the most rigorous traditions of native reasoning disregarded, even the latest views of modern science were blatantly ignored. As a result, modernity in India, to this day remains a 19th century construct weighed down by notions that Nehru imbibed in his days in Eaton and Cambridge ossified in his adulthood into a Fabian atheism that he foisted upon the Indian educational system being the first Prime-Minister.

Replacement of the Vedic Model of *Purusha* as *Angin* with *Angas* by the Guttenberg-Newtonian Model of Objectivity

In the traditional Hindu cosmology, the Universe was perceived as the body of the Being or *Purusha* and the parts of the Universe as his limbs. The human individual was part of the body of the *Purusha* even though the individual had its own body and limbs. Alternatively, the Universe was perceived as a Cosmic Egg (*Brahmaanda*) containing the individual. Whatever was contained in the individual was also perceived to be contained in the Cosmos (*yat pind.e tat brahmaand.e*) because the individual was also perceived as a *Purusha*, thus asserting a complete unity of the individual with the Universe. All Hindu ritual was conceived as a method of heightening the awareness of this unity in special as well as routine events, whether it was the ancient sacrificer/ worshiper (*yajamaana*) performing a Vedic oblation (*yajna*) inviting gods, or a modern individual entering a temple (which again represents the Cosmos), or the daily worshiper calling upon the gods to witness to a ceremony of birth, marriage or death.

There is a stark difference between this age-old Vedic method of performing an act before the Universe which is witnessed by the community, the gods and the demi-gods alike and the modern method of doing an act as a private action not witnessed by anybody. The first is ritual (*savana/ anushthaana/satra*) while the second is personal consumption or 'eating' alone (*bhukti*). The first was the prescribed (*vaidha*) way of life in traditional India and the second a forbidden (*nishiddha*) way. With the rise of Western individualism, the second becomes esteemed and normal while the first is seen as backward, abnormal or even suspect. In the Naturalistic Universe where there is no belief in any supernatural agency and Nature is a material for manipulation by the will of the individual, there is no reason to offer anything but every reason to take only.

Replacement of Orality with Writing

Philosophies and beliefs of a society depend on its educational system and the technology of their transmission. India used the aural as the main mode of knowledge preservation, although plastic, graphic and symbolic methods were not lacking. For instance, in spite of its prevalence from the time of *Sarasvati-Sindhu* civilization, writing was kept subsidiary to oral composition. Nowadays, there is an irrational presumption that Indian elevation of orality was caused by ignorance of writing. This is again based on the prejudice that graphicity once achieved can never allow orality to dominate. Hence the presumption that the *Sarasvati-Sindhu* script once lost, the very concept of a script was forgotten till reintroduced into India by the Greek and the Phoenician influences. The truth seems otherwise.

Orality, which was comprehensive enough to be a combination of speech (*vaacika*), *angika* (gesture), *saattvika* (mental concentraion) and *ahaarya* (symbolic dress) was preferred to other technologies of preservation as a cultural choice. This kind of orality keeps thought, speech, and action in a unity for performance in education, arts, rituals, and life in general. Whatever is to be done may thus be done by mind, speech and body (*manasaa, vaacaa, karmanaa*) together. This paradigm has operated on all aspects of Indian life. Hence the role of writing was made to remain supportive not performative in the culture. This paradigm also patterned India's educational systems.

The advent of Islam seriously disrupted the Indian educational systems and the institutions of all kinds of social and artistic performance. But it did not significantly alter the age old methodology of orality. It was for the British to usher in the new technology of print that played havoc with the systems of oral transmission. Two prejudices were established by the Europeans while assessing the value of Indian cultural products. One, that as a technology of communication, orality was inferior, inaccurate and untruthful and two, that the content of the Indian cultural messages of oral traditions was heathen and erroneous. Thus for the print oriented vision of the universe, orality was conceived as synonymous with pagan ritual (called *samskaraara/ savana/ anushthaana* in Sanskrit). For the colonial eyes, it was neither in form nor in content a vehicle of knowledge but of heathen misbeliefs, communicated through unreliable means. In general, the aural and thus the ritual, came to be associated with hoax, humbug, emptiness, externality, showmanship, deception and similar forms of untruthful pagan conduct. Only the objectively verifiable cultural products like manuscripts, sculptures, seals, metals or architectural remains could be claimed as genuine, truthful and perhaps even granted the status of the 'classical' if they compared well with the Greek examples. The colonial bias was reified in Independent India by the above mentioned Nehruvian 'scientific temper.'

Little wonder that the best way to declare one's Indian modernity is still to condemn ritual as deceit. This censure pervades not only the speeches of chest thumping social reformers, writers, poets, academics and journalists but just about anybody who is anxious to be called a citizen of his times. The habit stays strong. Talking about *Kumbha Mela*, in the *Hindustan Times*, January 20, 2001, Khushwant Singh says, "I fear crowds......I have met people who had been to such pilgrimages: they looked very pleased with themselves. But I did not notice any changes for the better in them. If they were prone to lying, cheating, backbiting, scandal-mongering, using bad language before they left for their holy cities or rivers, they came back and resumed lying, cheating, backbiting, scandal-mongering and using bad language. Truly had Guru Nanak spoken: *athsath teerath nahaaie utrey nahee maeil,* you may bathe at the 68 places of pilgrimage, it will not wash the dirt off your body (and mind). That does not deter the Guru's followers from doing precisely what he had castigated as a useless practice, or going to pilgrim centres".

This is the stock response of the Enlightenment Fanatics of the Nehruvian generation. They are out to denigrade ritual of any kind in the style of the British Utilitarians and Fabian Socialists. The malady is not restricted to the English medium expression but pervades a good deal of writing in Indian languages. Tomes can be found on elevating Kabir's verses against *saguna upaasanaa* (such as *'paahan puje prabhu mile to main poojoon pahaar.'*) and sundry cultural bureaucrats have lavishly rewarded musicians singing such showpiece *bhajans* thronging to which is a hallmark of progressive spirituality.

But the most amusing thing about these progressives is, that while they condemn the rituals of religion, they celebrate the rituals of the secular State like parades, prizes, ceremonies and celebrity parties with untiring addiction. Nehru set the example for this progressive hypocrisy by willing that his ashes be not consigned to the Ganges after a traditional Hindu cremation but to be taken in air and released all over India. It is doubtful if what he lost in the poetry of mantras was gained by that grandiose ritual.

It may be asked if rituals are the only methods that fail to alter the conduct of adherents. Books, the revered media of modern print culture are no guaranteed means of enlightenment. After all Kabir also said that people spend all their lives reading books but remain ignorant. (*Pothee para para jag muaa pandit bhayaa na koy; dhaayee aakhar prem ke padhe so pandit hoy*). One kind of spiritual or educational effort is as likely to fail as another. None is better than the other but is chosen according to taste by the practitioner. Results of educational pursuits are least measurable yet they are thought to be the best and most necessary investment in any society. The problem with Indian reformists and rationalists of all kinds, including the very early ones like Dayanand Saraswati, Ram Mohan Roy etc., was that they were not able to appreciate the complex variety of spiritual, educational and artistic methods that the Indian tradition has evolved over centuries to suit a variety of personal needs and urges (*'rucheenaam vaicitryaat riju kutila naanaapathajushaam nrinaam eko gamyah'*). There are various ways of cleansing the mind. But the rationalists of India, unaware of even the vast so called Western traditions of ritual cleansing like tragedy, procession and pilgrimage, are out to foist their narrow mind set on present day culture.

'*Samaadhi–Makbaras*' at Rajghat

Nothing reveals the duplicity of 'scientific temper' devotees shared and promoted by the Government of India than the show of ritual obsequity at the '*samaadhis*' or memorial shrines for the Indian Prime Ministers that stand in a long line at the banks of Yamuna in Delhi. Samadhi burial sites have been made for Hindu saints or Muslim sufis in India but never for kings. No memorial has been raised for a Hindu saint or a householder at the spot of cremation. The Indian ritual of cremation, unlike for other Indo-European ancients, contradicts the creation of a memorial building.

There was a scant justification to make a Samaadhi for Mahatma Gandhi, as he had been elevated to the status of an ascetic saint. But what is the logic behind the series of '*samadhis*' from Nehru onwards to all till the last dead prime minister (the latest though was shifted out of Delhi to Hyderabad)? Is it a new ritual that the rationalist secular State has forged by leaning on its Islamic heritage or on the modern Christian nations. The Rajghat memorials neither hark back to the grandeur of medieval edifices nor do they reflect the modern democratic spirit of equality. Why does the secular State ritually 'pray' on death anniversaries for the departed souls of its political leaders by appropriating a religious and spiritual practice that was reserved for *samadhis* and *makbaraas* of saints and sufis only? Clearly the 'scientifically tempered State' is simply confused about this.

Ritual is Planning Par Excellence

Need we point out that right from the Vedic period, the ritual mind has shown a capacity to plan meticulously not only the enactment of a spiritual rite but also a life higher ideals (*purushaarthadheeh*). For example in a *yajana,* the ritual performer aims at asking for a favor from gods, in which by correctness of procedure (*vidhi*) he ensures the result (*phala*). If ritual was some hocus pocus, its performers would not have developed so many arts and sciences that made the ancient Indian society so wealthy and satiated and at the same time philosophically adept to attract students from as far as China.

Ritual is Transformation not Repetition

Besides reinstating the myth that rituals are empty, the 'scientifically tempered' also allege that rituals are mechanical repetitions. Rituals seem so to the uninitiated and the unobservant. The rightly conducted ritual brings about a change in the doer's mental state, which is predictable, well tried, and permanent and not merely an autosuggestion or a hallucination. Controlling the mind in the entirety of its thoughts and feelings has been demonstrated and regularly applied in India in various fields like the arts, interpersonal relationships, social work, and spiritual pursuits. Throughout history, remarkable feats of character change and elevation have been achieved across the globe by the transformation wrought in individuals through ritual.

Modern consumerism infesting capitalist societies or Marxist states, use the same principles of mind control for serving the interests of greedy business corporations or tyrannical bureaucracies. The crucial difference is, a ritual is managed and performed by the individual out of his own free choice and taste and is beneficial to him, whereas State rituals serve national or corporate interest in which the individual may not be a beneficiary at all. Strongly nationalist, fascist or marxist states have therefore always disapproved, suspected or even repressed individual or special group rituals. The capitalist states may not do the same as they depend a lot on pampering the individual but they try to subvert individual ritualism by offering money spinning ritualistic events like Christmas sales, sports, Mothers' Day and so on. They are all opposed to individual transformation, as that can be a challenge to the State.

Ritual for Individual Sanity

It seems that in the 21st century, for a variety of reasons, the individual will find itself more and more cut off and lonely from the State, the family and the community as these units are becoming more an end to themselves and are doing less and less to nurture the individual. One of the ways the individual can nourish or renew one's strength is to choose one's personal rituals to transform the inner self for survival. As said earlier, rituals can be of diverse kinds, from the very mundane sort like feasting to the perfection of an art form, to an intense dedication to the spiritual. A conglomeration of happier individuals is a happier and more peaceful world.

Commandment-alization of Hinduism

Under the impact of colonial Christianity, Hinduism underwent a special phenomenon, which may be called as the 'Commandment-alization of Hinduism.' In India, this trend still continues even after independence as the Anglophonic ruling class has stayed under the sway of neo-colonialism. Some of the most deep-rooted prejudices against Hinduism that surfaced among the Islamic and Christian peoples when they first came into contact with Hinduism still prevail under the garb of many new fangled theories.

Two of these fundamental prejudices against Hinduism are caused by its worship of multiple gods and indulgence in rituals. These are seen as cardinal errors in contrast to monotheism and personal prayer elevated as the prime qualities of Abrahamic thought. In their hubris, the Abrahamics have not recognized that the Upanishadic Brahmavaada came to be evolved from the same tradition as the Vedic worship of multiple gods and is the oldest philosophy that propounds the unity of the Divine. For Christians and Muslims, the problem still exists as a divide between the people who believe in One omnipotent God and the people who admit the existence of many gods. The Abrahamic monotheists claim themselves to be logical and systematized and allege that polytheists are irrational and incapable of cosmic vision. It is primarily to address their false claim that one has to show that Hindus have thought on the subject more deeply.

The Naasadeeya Sukta of *Rigveda* gives the indication that there was somebody who created even before the gods came into existence. "Then was not non-existence nor existence; there was no realm of air, no sky beyond it. The

One, breathless breathed by its own nature; apart from it was nothing whatsoever." (*Rigveda*, Book X, verse 129). No doubt It/He/She was the *Purusha* of the Purusha Sukta. That One, alongwith the later well defined Brahma is what the Hindus have believed in. In this sense the unity of the Divine, behind all gods like Indra, Agni, Varuna, Mitra, Pooshaan. a, Usha and so many others of different manifestations is quite evident. '*Ekam adviteeyam*' (*Chandogya Upanishad*, 6-2-1) or '*Ishaavaasyamidam sarvam*'(*Ishopanishad*, 1), is the Hindu monotheism that admits also of material looking manifestations of the Divine.

As a matter of fact, Yahweh, Allah or Patera (God the Father) are endowed more with human attributes, basically those of the commanding father, than the Vedic Purusha or the Upanishadic Brahma. In the absence of the One taking anthropic morphe/*moorti*/ or the *saguna roopa,* Western monotheism has come to be riddled with virulent ikonophobia. In India this problem was resolved in the Vedic period if not before. While the Indian traditions have also admitted sects like Bauddhas, Jains, Paatanjal yogis, Gorakhpanthis, Kabirpanthis, Nakakpanthis, and the modern Arya Samajis, who do not pursue the path of morphic or '*saguna*' worship, it has not created the divide that the Abrahamics perceive.

The Indian philosophies that avoid the pursuit of manifested imagery have not denounced others as in falsehood and error. There is no reason, thus, why Hindus and the followers of Indic religions cannot call themselves believers in One (God morphic or a-morphic) and hence monotheists. While stating the unity of the Divine, they are not exclusivists as they do not admit that there can be only some manifestations/incarnations/characteristics of the One. The Abrahmic people are the exclusivists and as they insist that God can have only those characteristics as is found in Allah or Yahweh. The problem, then, is not One God versus Many Gods but God as seen by me alone versus God as seen by Others. The problem of the ineffable Ultimate One reality seen as diverse and as an image/icon/idol/anthropo-morphic '*moorti*' and vice versa was solved in India long ago, while other faiths of the world are still struggling or refusing to find an answer and hence are unappreciative of the idol worshippers and polytheists.

The Hindu faith in the Ultimate Reality behind all beliefs and philosophical systems is reflected nowhere better than in the benedictory verse of the play *Mahanatakam* by the eleventh century CE poet Hanuman.

" The One who is worshiped as Shiva by the *Shaivas,* as Brahma by Vedantees, as Buddha by Bauddhas, as Kartaa by Naiyayikas the logicians, as Arhat by the Jainas and Karma (*yajna*) by Meemaansakas; such a Vishnu, the lord of three worlds, may fulfil your desires".

The Abrahamic faith in its primary description of God as the Commanding Father has led to the elevation of his dictates as they have been revealed to the prophets of the tradition. For the Prophet alone there was seeing, knowing and hearing God, for the faithful, there are the commandments as revealed to the prophet. But for the Hindus, salvation does not come except by seeing and knowing oneself and not merely by following the commandments. Religion hence, in Abrahamic traditions has become co-terminus with the commandments in the Book, but for the Hindu it is a pursuit for realization.

With the dominance of these Abrahamic religions over the Hindus, there has been a mounting effort to reduce Hinduism to a set of commandments and take it away from its experiential content, which works through ritual and meditation. Those Hindu sects like Brahmo Samaj, Dev Samaj, Arya Samaj, Gandhism and the like, which were heavily influenced by Christianity have denigrated or eschewed Hindu ritualism and meditation and have assisted their debunking by Christians and Muslims. They have cloned a commandment-alized Hinduism and projected it as progressive and reformist and thus 'superior' to traditional Hinduism. However, while they have succeeded in promoting the Abrahamic point of view, they themselves as independent entities, slowly shrunk into mere movements of social reform, however laudable, and turned away from religious and spiritual enterprises.

Hinduism now needs to strongly resist this commandment-alization in order to save its original genius. It also means restoration of the unity of thought, speech and action which was broken by the other-wordly religiosity (*loka-paraangamukha Bhakti*), Euro-modernity, Protestant, Catholic and Islamic iconoclasm, and Gandhian dryness/ *rasaheenataa,* but is found as the ambrosiac kernel in the universe of pagan rituals.

In other words, what is to be revived is also the activity of the informed and conscious rituals and karma yogas. We have for too long fallen into delusions of believing, upholding convictions, mouthing them but doing nothing to realize them. The modern urban Hindu is often heard saying, "I believe in God, but I don't go to temples, I don't believe in rituals." If asked, "Do you do anything else, *dhyaana, bhajan, daana, sevaa,* whatever?" The answer often is, "No, that is all ritual, old stuff !" And to add insult to injury he/she looks upon ritual doers as backward people.

This is the illusion fostered by the print culture and the bookish education of the Macaulay-Nehru era. No action but just a rhetoric from the comfortable podium of a secure position. It is time to look at rituals, arts, social enterprises, sacrifices and journeys in a different way, as a unity of *manas, vak* and *karma* that restores the principles of pre-modern civilizations, except for some, almost all pagan, from North to the South Pole. Not only can they give us the philosophies and arts of integrated living but also provide lives of sharing things with earthly and divine beings.

2

Education Without Art

The Sahitya Academy each year awards Indian writers with a *taamra-patra* (citation on a copper plate) and a cash amount of Rs 40,000. If the copper is turned into gold by the Academy, the authors would gain something, but they would lose little if the cash is substituted by *paan-supaari* (betel leaf and areca nut). The Academy would at least succeed in making their awards purely honorable. So could the other academies for plastic and performing arts, namely the Lalit Kala and the Sangeet Natak, do well to follow suit. Why does the Indian State not declare that it cannot patronize the arts?

A good book or a song is indeed a priceless creation, but the one who creates it can be rewarded with a tangible recognition, which the aforesaid pittance hardly provides. That we have not thought of increasing this sum, at least 10 times, only speaks of the low esteem in which we hold creativity and the arts in particular. Our business corporations are no better as they have not even woken up to the idea that the mercantile world has a duty towards arts. They are not even aware that the *vaishyas* of yore were no lesser patrons of the arts than the kings. Nor have they learnt from contemporary Euro-American states where the government and the corporates invest heavily into education and art sustenance.

The biggest prejudice against the arts in India has been generated by its modern educational system that inculcates a diametrically opposite attitude to their worth as posited in the traditional Indian psyche. So-called makers of modern India, assiduously preserved the schooling system left by the British and only allowed the American educational jargon (propagated mostly by PL480 money financed professors) to modify the shape and size of text books leaving the content untouched. They have also maintained the hegemony of the printed word, the paper exercise book and the written examination over all other means of instruction and evaluation. Reading print and reproducing it in examinations remains the hallmark of our educational methodology. Our modernists have been so enamored of it that they are scared to consider another method, such as vocal expression, capacity to conduct reliable work projects, teaching of junior students by senior students and so forth. As a consequence, in this culture where the spoken word, intonation and gesture, signs, symbols and rituals had been developed as superb media of communication for thousands of years, now mere reading, cramming and reproducing prevails as the only method of passing examinations from nursery classes to the IAS. If the arts, except for music that still rests upon traditional training and Hindu ethos, have not touched great heights in free India, the sin lies at the doors of our education Ministers.

Ancient Respect for Creativity

The prime purpose of education is to ensure creativity in individuals. It is the best way to subdue their destructive instincts. When the ancient poet Bhartrihari said that a person without education is an animal (*vidyaa-viheenah pashuh*), he was not disparaging the animals, but showing the difference between the mentally innovative *homo sapiens* and the instinctively driven animals.

Societies with their immense variety are products of Man's mental creativity, not just of the gregarious instinct also found in lions and fish. Hence it was said by Aristotle, "man is a cultured creature" (*O anthropos politikon zoon*) wrongly translated under the impact of materialistic behaviorist theories, as "man is a social animal". Man the cultured creature continuously creates using his past for his future. Education is the methodology that ensures this creativity.

Societies, which are less emphatic about creativity, or are scared of it, such as ours at the present moment, tend to define learning in terms of short-term objectives. They value education systems by the materially productive work its students are likely to accomplish. They project role models of the glamorized achievers and preach competitiveness and survival of the toughest. Its jingles are: *jo jeetaa so sikander* "whosoever wins is Alexander" and "nothing succeeds like success" and so on. The Gandhian skepsis about means and end is already considered futile.

In the Indian, or rather in the Asian tradition, the trained (*samskrita*) or the educated individual has been the cornerstone of creativity, and hence of action and leadership. The notion of rustic simplicity, or lack of training as a mark of purity and naturalness, of the "mute inglorious Milton" is a Euro-Romantic concoction. In India, "*graamya*" (crude) or "*praakrta*" (natural) was regarded as impure, being untrained. However, the very notion of individualistic creativity in the whole of the ancient world was different from modern Euro-Romantic or post-modernist ideas of a shopper-like free floating self. Ancient individualism was rooted in community obligations and was meant to enlarge itself towards bigger entities.The *shloka* from *Mahabharata* quoted by me earlier was repeated in the *Kaakolooyikam* portion of *Panchatantra*:

> *Tyajedekam kulasyaarthe graamaarthe kulam tyajet Graamam tyajetjanapadasyaarthe aatmaarthe prithveem tyajet.*
>
> Give up the individual for the family, the family for the habitat, the habitat for the land. But for the Self, give up the whole earth.

Such giving up of "the whole earth" for the "self" really ends up in the self belonging to the whole earth, so different from the modern globalist-consumerist egocentricism. Also, the ancient "self"-seeker, was not always the *moksha* seeking wanderer, or the renouncer; he could also be a bread-earning family man, rooted in a village or city. He/she could be a creative "self"-seeker, pursuing any of the 64 *kalaas*, the arts, and could regard his pursuit as his liberation. After all, this has been the proclaimed faith of the Indian artist through the ages.

Art, no more Sacred

All this thinking has gone out of the modern Indian educational system. Art has come to be looked upon as nothing more than entertainment, whether refined or popular, highbrow or mass-mediotic. It is no longer sacred or liberating, *shubham* or *mokshadaa*. We have lost a major cultural faith and the fountainhead of our sustenance. The ancient Greeks too, regarded the non-utilitarian arts such as music, painting, poetry, dance, and theatre as builders of ethos (moral fibre). For this reason they made these an essential part of their educational system even for soldiers. But the modern West chose to discard this attitude. This idea was not considered worthwhile when Europe drew upon the intellectual inheritance of classical Greece. The arts though not dispensable, were only ornamental in the post Enlightenment education.

This thinking was imposed on India by the colonial educationists. What was worse, it was reinforced by the so-called Indian Renaissance by its fabricated picture of ancient Indian educational values. Puritanism, abnegation, and aggression were valorized in opposition to satisfaction (*tushti*), abundance (*samriddhi*), aesthetic softness (*laalitya*) and joy (*harsha*), which are described as a citizen's hallmark in our classical literature.

During the Independence struggle, and soon after, art was in effect, set aside by the puritanism of Gandhi, as much by the staunchness of Hedgewar, and the economic myopia of Jai Prakash Narain, Lohia and other socialists. The Marxists with their antireligious bias and their propagandist approach to art further damaged the traditional concept of sacredness and creative individualism in Indian art. Almost everybody presumed that India was too enslaved, poor and illiterate to think of art. Now that we are independent, the affluent among us are the crudest, even though the poor retain some traditional aesthetic sense.

Under the impact of Nehruvian scientific rationalism, the Government agencies responsible for making policy, curriculum as well as textbooks, like the National Council for Education Research and Training have been promoting a wooden version of science. There is an excessive emphasis on mugging "objective facts" about the physical world instead of imparting the skill of inductive logic. The quiz wiz-kids that every uppish school tries to produce are info-parrots only good for TV shows. Worst of all, in the name of modernity, contempt is planted in young minds for all the sciences and arts that prevailed before the Euro-Renaissance. Consequently our allopathic doctors have generally no dialogue with Ayurvedic or Unani practitioners; very few legal luminaries have acquaintance with ancient codified or customary laws; and not many physicists have studied ancient astronomy or music; hardly any modern psychologist has delved deep into theatre. The dichotomy between art and science, ancient and modern is made complete. Tagore and Aurobindo who presented healthy and exploratory methods to bridge this chasm were systematically marginalized and denigrated as too aesthetic or too spiritual by Nehruvian iron-jacket modernity.

Pop Art and Performance

Since the nineties, a vast expansion of television, films, advertisement and fabrics has created a new performance industry. This performance business is largely conducted through electronic and digital media which could have wonderfully harnessed the new technology to spread education and emotional health to every nook and corner of India at astonishingly low costs. But the result has been the opposite. The films have descended to sensationalism, the television channels to misinformation, advertisement to sweet lies, and fashion shows to flesh mongering. The Indian elite that manages this new media has no other interest than commerce. Education is furthest removed from the aspirations of this class. The whole enterprise apes the Western media and has failed to posit any values other than those of consumerism. It is like selling Mcburgers with coriander *chutney* as the only Indian content. This failure is not of means but of mind. Indians have come to accept the Western dictum that mass media can only have popular content, that is, it must descend to the lowest demands of taste. Any attempt to elevate and educate taste is considered anti-democratic.

The challenge before the Indian policy makers is how to create educational channels that provide attractive alternatives to crass commercialism. So far there is no thinking about it as the Indian political and intellectual elite is too colonized to depart from Western models of development. But a serious enterprise that forges the traditional elements of popular culture with modern social needs, can be both viable and elevating. The de-regulation of Indian television from State control and the monopoly of Doordarshan has seen the emergence of certain traditional discourse but only in the field of religions. India being a heavily religious culture perhaps thought of religions first of all. Let us hope that it shall think of art and social morality (*niti*) soon. And let us also hope that electronic media catering to religion and art shall not fall a victim to money making and power struggle. These channels like 'Samskaar', 'Aasthaa', 'God' could come into existence as religious *Gurus* and *Kathaakaar*s had an institutional existence independent of state patronage. But for educational channels to come into business is a remote possibility as all higher education is state financed. Private education at school level is also groaning under the yoke of state controls. Once there are a few dozen private universities and decontrolled education at secondary level, the emergence of educational channels on television and big digital publications would be a reality.

A concerted effort needs to be made to reinstate the arts as a creative, therapeutic and moral force in our educational system, print and electronic media. In schools the arts should be among the main subjects of study and not mere extracurricular activities. Five to six years of regular theatre classes in native language can develop clear speech, healthy and graceful carriage, and a direct familiarity with literature, myth and poetry in an easy way. It is more gracious and delightful than the present system of cramming through print. It has been demonstrated that theatre, dance, painting, and music are the best instruments of personality development for children. Why can there be no marking, promotion and academic recognition for them? Why have they been relegated to the lower category of 'vocational subjects' meant to be taken by duller kids?

When will we stop thinking of art as a handmaid of business, diplomacy, or infotainment and recognize it as an elevating experience that distinguishes humans from animals?

3

Shelving a Heritage

Sanskrit from Macaulay to M-Tv.

Nearly two thousand years ago, a poet commented on the Indian scene, "Intellectuals are engaged in envious quarrels, rulers are intoxicated by arrogance, the people are burdened with lack of education and so Good Speech is weak and emaciated." (*Boddhaaro matsaragrstaah prabhavah smayadooshitaa/ Abodhopahataashcanye jeernamange subhaashtitam*). It is not difficult to imagine that there have been repeated moments of darkness in our history. Mornings of needless debates in the Indian Parliament over the riddle whether it is secular or communal to perform *sarasvati vandanaa,* are not the first such spells of darkness. Else the lines of Bhartrihari as given above would not seem so contemporary. The ancient poet could make do with the word *subhashitam* or "good speech" as it was then an accepted synonym for "learning", "knowledge", *vani, vak,* or even *sarasvati.* There obtained then enough poetic taste to personify or deify speech, music or wealth. Long after Bhartrihari, even the Muslim poets sighed for God as the beloved and for a millennium, Turkish, Mongol, Taimurite, Afghan and Irani rulers (including Aurangzeb in his early life) enthralled themselves by patronizing court musicians singing Sanskrit and *brijabhasha* songs in praises of *sarasvati, naad* or *shabda.*

But this was well before the nineteenth century when Enlightenment came to us and we were bitten by the bug of secularist iconoclasm.

Miso-religious Secularism

The Indian people in general including Christians and Muslims would like that as a matter of cultural habit, any public conference, inauguration, convocation or opening begin with some kind of a thankful praise to the Divine (as was the custom of *mangalaacharana /svasti vaachana*) and end with a benediction for public well being (*aashirvachana*). But this is never allowed now as a Marxism infested secularity of the Indian State has imposed the principle of separation of State from the Church in the European and Soviet manner. Although the legal luminaries of *sarkaaree* patronage never tire of declaring that Indian secularism does not aim to look away from religious matters but only treats all religious denominations equally (*sarvadharmasambhaava*), in actual practice the Indian State mimics the West. A great uproar was created a few years ago when in a conference of education ministers of the various Indian provinces, an opening praise was sung for *Sarasvati*. In the conference, if it had been a matter of objection to preferential treatment to a Hindu goddess, there could have been a demand for including in the ceremony, verses in praise of the knowledge or the Word from the Bible, the Koran or the Granth Sahib. But the disease is deeper. Indian Secularism has taken the form of turning away from one's own heritage and disregarding the spiritual and ethical commitments that ancient and medieval vehicles of all religions and cultures symbolize. As a result, Sanskrit is the biggest casualty under secularist milieu. Practically speaking, secularism now means wallowing in easy consumerism of the day and neglecting religious and cultural issues. Hence the disruptive and not additive protests by the secularists. Unfortunately, the anti religious approach of the state policy has resulted in hurting us deeper.

Guilt for the 'Classical' Heritage

India alone excels in belittling its classical heritage as it has unfortunately codified it as its "Hindu past". This classification began in the colonial period when non-European cultures were primarily seen in terms of religious denominations of the non-Christian colored races. They were further divided into two broad categories, primitives (African, Australian and American aborigines) and statics (Asia and China). Within the Western world these approaches were countered first by Orientalists and later by Modernists, both not so enthused with Newtonian rationalism and the aura of cultural superiority it bestowed upon the European people. But while the Orientalists contributed to the discovery of the East by the West, they also succeeded in creating a somnambulist reassurance in the minds of many Indians who never tire of revelling in the praise of India by Schopenhaur, Max Müller, Blavatsky, Whitman and the like. In spite of the Orientalsits, administrators like Macaulay forged for India an education system which had little place, not only for Sanskrit literature, but for all the traditional arts and sciences like music, poetry, dance, theatre and painting, *Ayurveda, Rasaayan, Jyotisha*, metrics, etc.

This dichotomy continued well into the semi-century after independence and flourishes strong as ever. Even now, we have on one side Indologists, South Asian experts, Asian anthropologists, and ethnomusicologists etc., white, brown, black and yellow, native and foreign who would like a special treatment, almost protectionist, to be accorded to native cultures, and on the other hand we have the socialists, rationalists, scientificists, pluralists and globalists assured of the auto-built resilience and auto-generative capacity of native cultures. But neither side thinks that a formal educative system should have any role to play in the formation of culture. For them, as for Macaulay, culture can be extra-curricular. Indeed, it could be so for the colonizers who did not require culture for clerical/*babu*-work. But that it can be so for our future legislators, jurists, administrators, academics and scientists, is indeed a soft headed mushy belief that mocks the well known civilisational and educational principle that cultural values and behavior are not auto generative but need rigorous instruction.

The problem of giving Sanskrit its due place in Indian education is therefore, not just a matter of giving concession to a particular language. It is the task of using five thousand years of all the textual wealth produced in this subcontinent. And all who believe that these texts, the bulk being in Sanskrit, are not required for maintenance of cultural identity have little knowledge of civilisational rise and decline in history. Regarding classical heritage and Sanskrit, in particular, there are many misconceptions.

For instance, it is necessary to get rid of the notion (for some a phobia, for others a faith) that Sanskrit is the language of Hindus for promotion of Hinduism. This myopia of regarding the religious text as the only and paramount literature of a language is a syndrome extant among the colonized only. The European Christians created a great Renaissance from heathen Greek and Latin texts, which led them eventually to establish cultural equations with many other ancient languages and develop modern philology. Even now all Western universities have departments of classical studies, which provide crucial inputs to anthropology, philology and culture departments. Modern philosophical and scientific terms are still coined out of these two languages. But in India it is presumed that the study of Sanskrit, far from generating a utility for its texts along with those of *prakrits*, Persian and Arabic, will only result in their devaluation. So much for looking at history with religious spectacles only.

Arrogance of the Indian Anglophil

Indifference to Sanskrit and other classical languages is nurtured in no small measure by Indian Anglophils who live under the illusion that availability of ancient texts in English translations is sufficient for understanding the ancient ways of thought and feeling. For them there is no greater waste of time than learning ancient languages. Polyglossists are no longer admired in Indian academia. Indian universities do not demand a first hand knowledge of Sanskrit or *prakrits* from their doctoral researchers in history or philosophy. It is symptomatic of the times that a leading university like the Jawaharlal Nehru University did not have a Sanskrit department till 2002 although it boasted of having eminent historians on its faculty. The Indian Anglophones admire Orientalists but forget that the Orientalist enterprise was not to inform the Indian readers but to interpret a colonized culture for proselytization and governance. They also forget that no culture can do things for another culture; one has to seek meaning in one's own past by one's own effort. For those Anglophils that may doubt this even after Edward Said's work, one may remind them of T.S. Eliot's dictum that ancient text have to be studied and translated not only by each culture but also by each generation of a culture. So what great-grandfather Max Müller did for Europeans needs to be done by Indians for themselves today.

In a combative contrast to the Socialist, Secularist and Anglophilic berating of Sanskrit, there is the Hindutva dream that Sanskrit can be taught like a workout at the gymnasium. It is presumed that if pupils are subjected to its rote for five to seven years at school, the language shall be widely understood and read and even spoken in a couple of generations. There could be no surer way of doubling its pitiful state by making it a target of aversion of the common man who still holds the language in distant respect. Compulsory teaching may bring jobs to thousands of half-baked Sanskrit teachers who for a job will pledge allegiance not only to one political *Parivar* but to any other kind, dynastic, or otherwise. But they will not connect Sanskrit to contemporary life.

How to Revive Sanskrit

Sanskrit can happily be revived by enhancing the present day utility of ancient and medieval texts. The aim should be of bringing them in original and translation into the curriculum at all levels from school to college. This means a revision of the present curriculum and expansion of resources for inter-disciplinary participation. However, for the student, instead of compulsion there should be a wide choice to familiarize oneself with the traditional arts and disciplines. Theatre, music, poetry, medicine, *yoga*, *yogasanas*, aromatics, architecture, dance, philosophical concepts, etc., can be imbibed at school in easy familiar ways as so much of them still survive culturally. What needs to be terminated is the artificial gap created between the lived culture and the pedagogic role model of global yuppyism. It is here that these measures can be assisted by the electronic media to create a sense of Sanskrit as a living and not, what many are never tired of calling it, a dead language.

Some special awards and prizes need to be instituted that are truly high profile and Sanskrit specific only. Why hesitate in acknowledging that it is a special language as simply the volume and variety of its textual wealth far exceeds that of any other language on the globe? The present mentality of awarding *shloka* singing students and dumping shawls on the shoulders of some very aged pundits with insignificant money needs to be given up. Let there be awards for many achievements that relate to Sanskrit: for those who can deliver best software, for teaching it, to those who have written, published, edited and translated its texts, for those who have preserved it's Vedic *shaakhaas,* it's musical or dance compositions, or popularized it by teaching it far and wide.

All this requires is a sustained effort and careful planning to make classical learning and Sanskrit worthwhile rather than an object of pious obeisance. This can make it a useful passport for a sizable modern educated class of Indians to travel through many ages of their history and check things for themselves, having neither a glorified perspective of the past nor a contemptuous disregard for the artistic excellences and the sustaining wisdom of the pre-technocratic times.

4

Conversion: Sin or Sincerity?

The debate about conversion that ensued after a Papal visit of John Paul II to India, has touched many aspects of conversion such as, intellectual conviction of the convert, social mobility, improved respectability and the lure of money for the converted. However, some crucial facts about the spread of Christianity and Islam have been ignored.

The Papal call for the Asian Harvesting of Souls is no exercise to swell the coffers of the Church losing ground in the opulent West as many would like us to believe. It is based more on the notion that Christianity alone is the true religion while other religions are condemned to error. Even in a multicultural world, the Christian leadership does not wish to pluralize its dogma and offer it as, one more instead of, the only way to God! For the Pope, all religions may be equal but Christianity is more equal than others!

Apologies for Evangelism

Many cliches about conversion are kept alive by vested interests that prevent an evaluation of the evangelical agenda. The foremost being that conversion controversy is not a religious issue but a vote-catching device. It is projected as a Hindu Conservative Right versus Progressive Left confrontation. But time has shown that proselytization is not a battle for votes, but a battle for souls with a long history of cultural beliefs and behavior patterns that goes far beyond the smaller fortunes of the Nehru or the Sangh Parivar.

Another cliche is that conversions have always been a result of the low caste Hindus turning to other faiths to escape the oppression by higher *varnas.* Christian and Muslim evangelists are never tired of projecting their faiths as truly egalitarian and democratic based upon the ability to provide equal opportunities to all their adherents irrespective of their birth or social class or caste. Abrahamics are said to provide a God who looks upon all men as equals, unlike Hinduism where birth based classification of caste/*varna/jati* makes some men lesser than others in the eyes of humans as well as God. Once born in low caste, there is no change possible in a life time. A Hindu, it is said, can only be reborn in higher caste, if at all he is lucky and is not born as an animal or insect. Conversion, hence, is the shortest, sweetest and surest way of achieving equality. As the Hindu clergy does not preach egalitarianism but reinforces caste hierarchy as an article of Hindu faith, they are guilty of pushing Hindus towards conversion. The Shankaracharyas and Hindu rightists are held responsible for maintaining caste and not declaring that there is no authority even in the Vedas for birth-based *varnas*, says the guilt ridden modernized Hindu. It is said that if non-rigidity and upward mobility of caste takes place, it shall bring a Hindu reform and stop the "one-way traffic of conversions to other religions". This palliative has deluded a vast amount of modern Hindus with reformist convictions.

Strangely enough, these Hindu progressives are themselves very shy to define "reform". Do they mean doing away with caste altogether or only providing greater mobility to the lowest rungs through affirmative action? Or do these progressives wish to give a new definition of *caturvarna* by modern professions through *guna* and *karma*, or yet some other formula? The Congress is as timid as any other party in starting a caste-clastic movement. Though such a movement is much needed to modernise and truly democratise Hindu society, such a movement shall not provide any security against conversion conflicts.

As a matter of fact, caste has little to do with conversion. No Muslim or Christian convert of low caste forgoes his caste and gains a status of even workable equality with upper caste Christians or Muslims. If it was so, Churches of all denominations would not be demanding reservation for Christians on caste basis. The motive to become Muslim or Christian was seldom freedom from caste hierarchy. For vast populations it was always either force or allurement of economic uplift, for stray individuals it has been anything from philosophy to sex.

When Christianity arrived in India in the first century, the caste-system had become quite rigid. If Christianity was such a relief for the underdogs why did it not grow in leaps and bounds from its very arrival? In early centuries, let alone in India, in the Mediterranean as well, Christians were not focussing upon the destitute entirely to multiply their fold. They influenced the highly placed sections of the Roman and Greek bureaucracy and their great expansion came only after the baptism of Constantine, the Roman Emperor.

In India, Christianity remained in isolation till the Protestant British gave it an impetus, keeping at bay even the older Orthodox Christians. Similarly, Islamic rulers did not target the lower-caste Hindus who were incapable of effectively supporting the Turkish, Afghan and later Mughal elite. They left these poor neoconverts to Sufis whom they seldom patronised and often persecuted as potential spokesmen of the poor. An unabashed instigator of proselytisation, the historian Ziauddin Barni advised the Sultanate to target the Brahmin intelligentsia and the big Hindu landowners and merchants to be cowed into submission and conversion.

The ruling Muslims in India never objected to the *varna-jaati* hierarchy as they themselves believed in social status by birth, distinction between lord and slave, *ashraf*, *arjal* and *ajlaf*. The elite class that belonged to the royalty and military eminence were *ashraf* that included Qureshi, Jafri, Hussaini, Alvi, Osmani, Farooqi, Siddiqi, Saiyads, Moghuls, Naqvi, Zaidi, Kazmi, Rizvi, Hashmi, Abbasi, Arabs, Pathans, Sherwani, Shairazi, Isphani, Timizi, Bukhari, Qazi, Mullick, and Mirzas, etc. They were originally foreigners and some of them even boasted of 'blue blood' as they were able to import Central Asian women. During the days of the Islamic rule in India, they were the high and mighty and even when they married the Hindu princely women whom they converted to their religion and manners, they were known as torch bearers of the clans they originally belonged to before settling in India, The converts to Islam from the Indian artisan, trading and agricultural classes were called *ajlaf* and were the new middle class of Islamic population in India, who were semi respectable like the Ansari, Mansoori, Mirasi, etc. The lowest category that converted from the Hindu *shudra* classes were called *arjal* and did not take up any Arabic caste names and continued to be known by their professions such as *dhobi, halal khor, dhuniya, dom*, etc. To this day the matrimonial columns of the Muslim community reflect this divide. The Hindu hierarchy was conveniently used to reinforce Muslim hierarchy. It is in the very late period, nearly towards the dusk of the Mughal rule that a larger number of the low-caste Hindus converted to Islam as they were sucked in by the economic allurement of preferential treatment to converts.

Conversion for Colonization

The belief that all humans are born equal was given as a social agenda only after the Industrial and the French Revolutions. But much before that proselytsing was used by the Christian colonialists to almost entirely convert followers of traditional religions belonging to agrarian , hunting and forest societies of the American, African and other continents to integrate them into the colonial set ups through the overt and covert push and pull of "education and medical care" (which could also be called initiation into industrial consumerism and allopathy from erstwhile simpler economies and herbal medicine).

In the modern era, conversion to Christianity means both a well-planned degree of ubranisation and "Westernisation". The ancient Indian Hindu or medieval Hindu ruling classes had no such needs nor any expertise to enter deep forests or hills to widen their civilisational ambit. Hence, the VHP reconversion bids are crude as compared to the subtle cultural penetration perfected by the Christian evangelists in the name of modern education and health services.

It is not totally true that the primary motive of Christian missionaries of any denomination is to improve the standards of life for the poor, the marginalised and the aborigines. If this was so, vast populations of the South American and the African continents would not be living even after conversion in poverty and exploitation by the rich Christian West. For most converts, the health and education programs of the Church are only up to the point of baptism. Nor it is true that any kind of serious intellectual or spiritual persuasion goes into the act of taking the simpler folks into the fold. A mix of medicine and faith healing demonstrating the power of the new God and his Son, is employed. To take an example from the tribal areas of the Dangs of Gujarat itself, as admits a researcher Mr. Irfan Engineer, "If the *bhagat* could not help him/her get rid of the evil spirit, which the Adivasi believes is the reason for his/her disease and the Christian prayer could, he/she prays , in addition to all *Dev*s, to *Yesudev* or *Esudev* whose superior power over the spirit has been demonstrated" (The Hindu 23.1.99). Such tactics reveal that the objective is to achieve targets of numerically successful proselytisation.

It is strange however, that some Indian liberals approve of the route of Christian assimilation of tribals into urban culture but condemn the Hindu route to urbanisation. And this notwithstanding the fact that tribal religious practices of possession and animism are closer or identical with many Hindu practices but have always been anathema in Christianity. The trauma that tribal societies face through either route and the deprivation they go through both ways seems to be nobody's concern. The ancient urbanites were less presumptuous as their powers of penetration were limited.

Another cliche on conversion is that it has always been going on in India. Some historians very gleefully point out that followers of the Vedas have been changing to Buddhism,

Jainism or Tantrism and vice-versa. This perception overlooks the fact that such conversions merely meant sectarian transition. They required no cultural transitions of language, music, or basic rituals of life and death. Above all the rock-bottom common Indian beliefs of reincarnation, world as transient suffering, doctrine of karma, acceptance of the divine both as icon and formless, and belief in final knowledge through a supra-mental experience, remain unchanged. For a Shaivite, a Vaishnavite is different, but not damned and is not needed to be saved from heathenism or *kufra*. Proselytising is not a sacred duty and martyrdom no sure way to salvation. The inter-mixing of beliefs, rituals and practices of various denominations in India is ample testimony to that. Even now, when Hindu preachers make adherents of yoga and meditation in the West, only a few insist on relinquishment of the earlier faith. Intermixing is, in fact, encouraged as an article of new faith.

Conversion to Islam or Arabization?

There are so many claims made by the proponents of Islam regarding its egalitarianism, caste-less-ness, universalism, peacefulness, and even victim-hood at the hands of the West. These have to be openly examined and tested before the mounting evidence against these claims. In fact, the industry for Islamic apologetics is as big and well financed as is the endeavor of the globally spread out violent jihad. It has infiltrated the best universities and research institutes of the West and maintains an independent network of Islamic centers world over that nourish an intellectual resistance to a long overdue reformation in the interpretation of the canonical texts of Islam. A Reformation, of the kind that occurred in Christianity and brought it out of the Middle Ages, is thus indefinitely postponed. Vast populations of Muslims are denied the benefits of modern thoughts and life-styles.

Except for the manner of the assembly for prayer, the *namaz,* in which there are no special places or visible hierarchy, there are few things in Islamic life that can be taken as based on egalitarianism or equality of treatment for the faithful. The severe subjugation of women is the most glaring example of the inherent belief of Islam in inequality that is enshrined as the unchanging and un-compromising world of God. Not only the rights of the non-believers, but of half of the faithful, the women, are so severely restricted, that the very thrust to seek freedom from codes and manners that are outdated and detrimental is smothered. Islam creates a self-enclosed world in which there is only admission (sanction by force as well) but not the right of exit. Leaving Islam is regarded as punishable by death and marrying a non-Muslim also invites penalty. Egalitarianism in Islam is thus a very distant dream, if at all possible.

We have already mentioned the caste hierarchy among Muslims based on the tribes of Arabia that gives a lineage to Indian Muslims right from the time of the invasion of Muhammad bin Kasim in Sindh to the present day. Of these the elite class of *ashrafs* mentioned earlier, is as closed and inbred as are the orthodox Hindu Rajputs or Iyers. Nobody, however rich and educated, would be admitted to an *ashraf* tribe/caste if he converts, unless it is a she who marries an *ashraf* male. The bulk of the conversions to Islam are from the very low castes, mostly *harijans,* who retain their earlier names like *dhobis, chamaar* etc, and join the *arjal* category of yore. Present day politics of some Muslim leaders pleading for 'muslim-dalit' unity is another ploy to increase the fold of Islam and has nothing to do with empowerment or betterment of converts. The Congress and the Left parties gunning for extending the benefits of reservation available under the present Constitutional laws to the scheduled-caste and scheduled-tribe Hindus to the Muslim converts recent or age-old, are actually playing into the hands of proselytizers. How can Islam (or Christianity) the so called 'egalitarian' religion(s) ask for benefits if there is nobody considered low in its ranks?

The fact remains that traditional Islam envisages a perpetual colonization under its theory that divides the world into two, believers in Islam or the *umma* and the infidels (*kafirs*). From this follows another division about the nature of the State, which can be only of two kinds, either an Islamic theocracy (*dar-ul-islam*) or a government of the infidels (*dar-ul-harb*). Classical Islamic thought cannot reconcile with the idea of any third kind of the State, Whether secular, multi-religious or pluralistic. The non-Islamic State must be converted into an Islamic State by converting its population into the *umma*. It is for this reason that it is also called the 'area of war'. Thus the endeavor for conversion becomes a holy duty.

Since the flushing of petro-dollars in the Gulf States, particularly in the Kingdom of Saudi Arabia, a literalist Islamic movement called Wahabism has chosen to culturally de-localize the Muslims all over the globe. Wahabism or Salafism promotes an acceptance of the supremacy of Arab culture by pushing the Shariat laws, denial of education and freedom of movement to women, enforcement of the veil on women and their acute segregation, promotion of a peculiar sartorial style, creation of a parallel education for Muslims based on the *Quran, Hadith* and *Sunnah,* and the injection of Arabic vocabulary into other languages. The cultural impact of Wahabism thus is anti-eclectic and anti-pluralistic. Politically it juxtaposes the *umma* against the national loyalties of a Muslim citizen. In recent years militant Islam has succeeded in creating several new political states under the above-mentioned strategy. The new states of Pakistan, Bangladesh, Kosovo are some examples and imbroglios like Kashmir, Chechnya and others are the 'areas of war' with uncertain fate and miseries unending.

Both Christianity and Islam have carried a special burden of saving souls and used the opportune moments of political patronage to expand drastically. These religions are exclusionist as they do not like to mix norms of worship and social conduct with other faiths. The huge and rich outfits for proselytizing that both maintain globally cannot be ignored. By now their methods have centuries of experience behind them. To hold its ground Hinduism can deal with them only through dialogue and discussion, violent confrontation being the worst way as it shall give proselytizers the status of healers. Even token "reconversion" campaigns are ill-advised as they make a mockery of religious faith.

5

Bring Back the Teacher

It is worth noting that the university system in India has hardly changed since colonial days. Now after more than sixty years of freedom we should have the courage to identify the implanted deficiencies in the present system of education and to revive and contemporize the concepts that once worked in the indigenous system to produce great excellence.

Most of us forget that for almost a millennium, India maintained a system of higher education, which was availed of by many neighboring civilizations, including China. This traditional system, of *guru* and *gurukul*, centered entirely on the teacher and his direct relationship with his disciples. It was rigorous and demanding and yet flexible. It used emotional ties to create long-term obligations and accountability. In spite of its hierarchy, it had an admiration for the individual excellence (*pratibhaa*) on the basis of which sometimes very young persons were elevated as head-teachers, or *achaaryas*. Recognition of talent is a phenomenon that seems to have disappeared in modern India. In the traditional system of education pedagogy was looked upon not as an instrument of knowledge but as a catalyst. Epistemologically, it considered teaching as "awakening" and not as "transference" of knowledge based on "course-work". The student was regarded not as a clean slate, but as a seed to be nurtured by the psychic ability of the teacher whose methods were flexible and suited to the individual student. In the traditional system the teacher was a free decision maker in his realm. Despite the obligatory support by the state and the community close to the location of the ashram, monitoring of teaching institutions was distant and indirect. In brief, the teacher was trusted and left alone.

Teacher Out Administrator In

Western pedagogy ushered two major changes. It not only brought in print technology to replace the oral Indian method, and it also removed the teacher from the center and brought in the academic administrator. The European system derived from the paradigm of the Christian seminary where the emphasis was on the learning through regimen. The ecclesiastic head here was more of an administrator and less of an intermediary between the novice and knowledge. From this example, the European University system came to focus on course work, which was taught and tutored, but never considered to be "revealed" by the teacher. A collective body gave the final degree. In short, the personal bond between the student and the teacher, the psychic nurturing, which existed in the Indian or in the Greek tradition, did not obtain in Europe.

The British tinkered with the idea of "Oriental education" before enforcing their own system. Apart from its educational content, methodology and technology, "Oriental education" would have been unacceptable to the British, as it would have retained the primacy of the indigenous teacher, the traditional notion of the *achaarya* who was beyond their ken. So instead of introducing new learning into the indigenous set up, they preferred to promote institutions in which the teacher was made a cog in the wheel. The system revolved around the principal in the school, the vice-chancellor in the University, the director or the academic administrator, in a research institute. All of these were directly appointed by the State. This was unthinkable in traditional India, even in the period of Islamic governments. Before the British, the governments never appointed the teachers but only supported them through charity.

During the struggle for independence, many institutions were founded and supported by non-governmental trusts that worked with exemplary zeal for the promotion of nationalism and indigenous ideas. But in post-British India, public keenness to invest in education eroded overnight as it was presumed that the new Socialist State should be able to shape a fresh system more responsive to national needs. This proved to be a tragic error. The state, while it took upon itself totally to bear the burden of education, did little more than preserve the colonial set up aimed at producing graduates to fill the ranks of its Socialist bureaucracy.

Imitative Socialist Model

During the period of Independence struggle the major issue in the field of education was the difference between colonizer and the colonized. There was a great desire to define a system of education and the content of education that would be suitable to India's heritage as well as her present needs. A good deal of thought was given by some of the most eminent Indians to distinguish and contrast India from the West in terms of civilizational values. The free country was to adopt something for its own needs rather than to continue with the colonial habit. But no sooner the power came to the hands of Indians themselves, headed by Nehru they craftily replaced the dichotomy between the indigenous and the colonial by a self created dichotomy between the Hindu majority and the Muslims and Christians which were looked upon as the main minorities (the other minorities like the Sikhs, Jains, Buddhists were newly imagined as non Hindu and hence declared as minorities). Hence the real issue of removing the colonization was shelved. The country got involved in a divisive conflict in the name of protecting religious rights of the minorities from a perecived threat by the Hindu majority. This syndrome eliminated the teaching of religious concepts and ethics in the name of secularism. This secularism was no more than a carbon copy of watered down Westernization. As most of these models from the West are meant for middle class societies, in India, neither at the college nor at the school level they succeeded in providing efficient and quality education.

Even those Christian and Muslim institutes of higher education that had earlier nurtured their students with anti-colonial feelings now shed their modernizing agenda and under the control of bishops and imams worked to make their reputation as preparatory schools for the Indian Administrative Service and upper division clerks or lately for producing good techno-coolies.

The new political echelons and the bureaucracy magnified the stranglehold of the socialist state over higher education to unthinkable proportions. From appointments of vice-chancellors and promotions of teachers, setting admission policies and student fees, the functioning of the universities fell exclusively into the hands of political lobbies.

There was no possibility of the intelligentsia asserting themselves, as political infiltration of the teacher and student ranks became the order of the day with the unions acting as over-anxious brokers.

This was a grievous betrayal of the rebellion voiced against colonial education during the freedom struggle. The new bureaucracy, with a Euro-derivative mindset, eschewed all indigenous models of Gandhi, Vinoba, Aurobindo or Tagore and invited the Western second raters to devise jargons as opiates to our academia because indigenous models while opening all doors for modernity of curricula, affirmed the centrality of the teacher-figure, an anathema to our *neta-sahab* duo.

Decontroling Education

The first step towards freeing higher education is to establish that the State is obliged to support but not to define education. Neither legislators nor administrators are trained to select and appoint educators or to prescribe the content of education. Let us not forget, that this was not so in this country even in the days of monarchy. The powers of mass-persuasion, once the domain of the intellectual class, are being used in the name of democracy by the legislature. The intellectual class must now free value and opinion making institutions from the clutches of legislators. The philosopher must check the king.

Hence, major amendments are needed in Acts of all universities to prevent the installation of army generals and IAS officers as vice-chancellors by Prime Ministers and Chief Ministers. The consultation and concurrence of the apex bodies of the universities should be mandatory under law before the approval by the chancellors, President of India or chief ministers of the States. The chancellors should have the power to interfere only in genuine emergencies. Like the judiciary, teacher-committees augmented by proven artists and scientists should do teacher appointments at all levels.

A national opinion must be created to persuade all political parties to wind up their now openly maintained wings in student and teacher unions. The senates and academic councils of universities should have fewer legislators as representatives and more of teachers. In the last decade it has become crystal clear that teacher unions are split along political lines and do more squabbling than good. The teachers must also give up their allergy to business representatives in councils and invite donations from the industry. The teacher-turned-administrator basking under political patronage must go for good.

Corporate Funding and Donation for Education

A major shift has also to be effected in the source of support. The responsibility of funding education, particularly higher education, should not and cannot lie exclusively on the government. As said earlier, State was not a heavy supporter in any period in India. It is the modern socialist misadventure that has given total control of education to the legislator. Nor is crass commercialization an option that seems to fascinate many votaries of globalization.

The success of private schools for the middle class which are in a very huge demand has encouraged profit makers to join the education industry. The most disturbing truth revealed by a survey that massive amounts of bribes are paid by Indian parents for admissions of their wards. If on one hand this is corruption, on the other, it is indicative of a cultural aspiration for knowledge so well inculcated by tradition and used for elevating the quality of life. The former should be removed and the latter preserved. Any attempt at a commercial reductionism will be disastrous in the long run as it will create social strife. The education system needs to be made for not just the tuition paying middle class but others as well. With a huge poor population, India needs to train its young poor to learn modern and technological labour skills so they can graduate to middle class status and good employment at a global scale. The Euro-American model in which the student takes loans and makes service bonds works well only for middle class societies with slim family ties.

Hence, the nation needs to urgently devise extensive charitable support for the poor but deserving students. It is at this point again that the legislator class has created a needless conflict between the deserving poor student and the undeserving not at all poor who claims concession on the basis of his caste or religion. Instead of following the simple rule of offering unstinted help (through state, corporate or other charitable funding) to the needy but promising student of whatever caste, creed, gender or religion, the legislative classes have cunningly crafted a system of vote banking in which promises are made to the ever expanding 'backward castes' and minorities in return for electoral support. The lone teacher is increasingly exasperated today by the never ceasing newer categories of students that are made his charge by 'virtue' of their birth and least of all by their competence and skills. Teaching the merit-less is the biggest oppression that the Indian teacher now increasingly faces, something his predecessor was spared under kings and colonizers.

Reservation, Blight or Blessing?

Educational institutes flourish or flounder simply on the basis of the competence of their students and faculty. This is true for all times, whether for simple Indian ashrams of yore that subsisted on a hand to mouth agricultural patronage or for the modern universities that are equipped with nuclear cyclotrons for high technological research and are funded by the state or rich patrons. Nothing can replace competence to learn which must be ensured in the students at the time of admission. Students endowed with these qualities alone are the truly deserving ones. While one may not discriminate among learners on the basis of class, creed or social status, no institution can survive if it admits as many dullards as the clever ones on the basis of generosity to the poor or the disabled. The present day hotly pursued doctrine of compensatory discrimination called reservation or affirmative action, that identifies certain groups in a given society to be given preferential treatment for admission even at the expense of the highly meritorious, has created a major crisis for the pursuit of excellence in institutes of higher learning.

With the retreat of socialism the legislative class of India is fast losing the power to distribute economic and culture benefits in all spheres. In order to continue their dominance as the distributor of goodies, the legislators have now invented the reservation game as a fading shadow of their socialist clout. As all Indian universities are state financed, either by the Center or the States, the legislators wish to make them a venue of struggle for admissions on the basis of caste, creed, religion, poverty and perhaps some other criteria that will elude rationality. The Schedule Castes and Tribes were given reservation in Constitution, to which the category of OBC (other backward castes) was added in the eighties. But the search for categories that can be regarded as backward or the lowest, and have been perceived to suffer at the hands of the upper castes, is still on.

Unlimited Categories for Reservation

The amount of reservation and the kinds of people that are clamoring to be in the reserved category is already close to the ridiculously high. The Supreme Court has already ruled that no more than 50 percent of the admissions available can be put in the reserved category. But this norm has been flouted and the legislators are attempting to make it as high as 80 percent, a situation that already prevails in Tamil Nadu. In a spate of vengeful thinking against the upper castes, demonstrated merit and competence has been long discarded. The legislative game of dangling the carrot before their electorates has already made educational affirmative action in India, a laughing stock before the world. "Vote me to power and I shall ensure your wards get into colleges at a high concession in merit standards, and if they later join the youth wing (the lumpen muscle men) of my party so much the better for their future," so goes the refrain of the song of what is now being called social justice.

Creating newer categories of people who can be declared eligible for reservation is the reckless game that the legislative class is now playing freely. Seeking to amend the Constitution that does not presently allow reservation on religious grounds, politicians are now pushing for Muslims to be included in this category. Very soon there will be a demand for Sikhs, Buddhists, Bahais and Parsis to be put in the reserved category. Once the religious minorities are included in the reserved category, the category of religious minorities itself will be enlarged. The Congress is already gunning to define the Jains as minorities. Its success shall open the floodgates to many claimants like Radha Swamis, Lingayaats, Brahmakumaaris, Arya Samaajis, Kabirpanthis, Sai baba panthis and to a dozen other sects that are today placed in the ambit of Hinduism, to be declared as non-Hindu independent minority religions.

The erstwhile ruling of the Supreme Court denying the status of the non-Hindu minority to the Rama Krishna followers, may undergo re-examination and the above mentioned sect may end up claiming an independent non-Hindu status. Logically, it is difficult to argue that if the Sikhs (Nanakpanthis) believing in the doctrine of one formless Supreme Being (*eka nirankaara*) and the doctrine of Vedanta as explained by Nanak can be declared as non-Hindu, then why the Kabir Panthis believing in the same formless Supreme Being and the same Vedantic tenets, as pointed out by Kabir cannot be declared a non-Hindu? Perhaps, sensing the massive Pandora's Box soon arriving on its table the Supreme Court has observed that there should be sooner or later an end to reservation and a date should be fixed from when the affirmative action shall cease to be a state obligation.

However, for the present, Indian legislators have propagated admission to college as the surest short cut to social climbing for the backwards. In reality, even when that is secured and a degree is obtained, the paucity of jobs in the market and the poor standard of education caused by the flooding of universities by incompetent and aimless students, results in the creation of armies of the employed. Thus, even reservation, is defeated in its aim of securing skills and jobs for the poor and socially disadvantaged.

Create Competence not Reservation

The policy makers should give up the chimera of reservation, which has plunged the nation into dangerous social strife, and concentrate instead on facilitating competence among the needy. Contrary to the propaganda, there is no shortage of resources or will among the people of India. It is the insistence of permit-raj addicted politicians to keep education under their thumb that has prevented huge funding from the people to be poured into education. In the earlier pages we have given the method that could be followed to decontrol education at all levels, from the basic to the higher kind.

The institutions of higher learning should be left alone to admit the competent and the meritorious students only. For those who on account of economic backwardness, caste disadvantage or soçial isolation are unable to secure admissions in open competitions, there should be special educational facilities assisted, managed and financed not only by the state but by the people themselves. Training aspirants for special examinations is already an industry not only in India but world over. Coaching schools for the Indian Administrative Services, medical, engineering and other colleges are doing roaring business all over. If this activity is turned into an educational and philanthropic service, the genius of the disadvantaged boys and girls shall have a great chance to flower.

Some sterling efforts by enterprising persons have shown

the way by which financing children of the poor to join special coaching centers can result in the students making their way to the highest institutions through competition. The Dakshina Foundation, organized by an imaginative NRI, discovered that Kota in Rajasthan has emerged as the top town where preparation for entrance examination of Indian Institute of Technology is an industry by itself. Every year some 30,000 aspirants from all over the nation go to reside in Kota. Rooms are available for Rs 3,000 a month or so with three meals a day. The tutoring institutes are all-for-profit and charge Rs 40,000–90,000 per year. As more than one-thirds of the total incoming class of IIT freshmen is from one of the Kota institutes this industry has achieved a stunning success. The Dakshina has contracts with the best five of institutes who coach the Dakshina scholars. Dakshina covers the entrance test taking costs as well as their coaching and residential expenses of promising candidates. These successful scholars, after acquiring good jobs contribute to Dakshina for life to help others. Another case is of the super boys of a 'Super 30' coaching institute in Patna located inside a small thatched house with fraying wooden benches and creaking tables in a densely populated lower middle class locality. At Super30, twenty-eight of thirty pupils have passed the IIT entrance test this year. They all come from poor families and from Hindi medium institutions or little-known English medium ones. Their education is totally subsidized.

These exceptional cases only point out the way for providing assistance to brilliant poor students, irrespective of their caste or creed. If Indian society is now geared to the creation of such assistance, a healthier educational infrastructure based on excellence and equality shall emerge in which the beneficiaries shall always hold their head high and help others to gain knowledge.

The so called public schools in India that are largely schools for the middle and upper middle class children can also be asked to admit a substantial percentage of students from the disadvantaged classes. In fact there is a standing order of the Supreme Court (case of *Modern School Vs Government of India and others*) directing schools to follow all the conditions laid down by the government while granting any form of aid. This meant not just a cap on the fees but also reserving 25 percent seats for poor students and funding their education. Reservation if at all is required at the primary school level. It should be looked upon not so much as affirmative action but as a responsibility of the wealthier to assist the poor.

The order that the apex Court issued for the schools in Delhi could be extended to the whole of the country. And if it is implemented the number of economically weaker children going to the so called public schools would be staggeringly large. This single measure adopted sincerely is enough to eliminate the need for affirmative action in institutions of higher education. The children of the poor would have had the opportunity to prepare themselves at the very primary level. But this and similar measures do not interest our politicians as there is no scope of dangling carrots before the electorates.

Funding for education has to be shared by the people through voluntary donation and support. It is a mistake to think that corporations, business houses and wellfare bodies will not be willing to share the burden. They would want to do so but they will also like to have a share in the governance and policy making for creating systems and curricula that suit the immense plurality of India. They would also wish to have tax holidays and permanent concessions for funding. It is at this point that a firm resolve is needed to eliminate the legislative monopoly. In brief, it is again the problem of dismantling state controls. The nation freed of legislative clutches will witness flowering of learning as was seen when Europe came out of the shackles of the Christian church and freed learning to produce new sciences and the industrial revolution.

The nation must again repose its faith in the teacher. This may sound like asking for the moon. But if after half a century it can be realized that state control has stifled national economy, that supremacy of the legislators in appointing judges can endanger the freedom of the judiciary, surely there can be rethinking on the role of the teacher who deserves the freedom to be what he is, a maker of minds.

KULA : Broken Homes

6

Yayatis and Kamsas

Unbridled Indulgences of Affluent Indians

Yayati, stands out in the *Mahabharata*, as a king who never tires of talking obedience to *dharma*. He is scared of the authority of the *aacharyas*, but will not resist the smallest opportunity for sensual gratification. He rescues Devayani from the well but dares not accept her offer of marriage till approved by her father Shukracharya. When the *acharya* agrees, Yayati asks for a decree absolving him of the sin of cohabiting a woman of higher *varna,* that is forgiveness to him as a *kshatryia* for marrying a *brahmin's* daughter. He is happy to accept along with Devayani, the princess Sharmishtha, who was made a life-slave of Devayani by her father, and the two thousand maids that served Sharmishtha. Even though forbidden to cohabit with Sharmishtha, he could not resist for very long, knowing well the inevitable wrath of Shukracharya. When cursed into old age, he asks leave of Shukracharya to ask for youth from his sons promising in return his kingdom in inheritance to the son who gives his youth. His son Puru agrees, and with that borrowed vigor, Yayati enjoys all pleasures with the apsara Vishvachi for a long time. He returns, though still unsatisfied, to hand back the youth to his son, Puru. His last and only likeable act is the enunciation that no amount of indulgence can ever satiate a man.

Kamsa, his story too well known, is epitome of the power usurper turned into an uncontrolled tyrant. Enjoyment of power through violent aggression was his mode. Collateral damage is inevitable when such beings occupy thrones. Their rule leaves behind a memory of extensive violence. Yayati, on the other hand, is a man who overstrains to stay on the right side of *dharma* and yet fulfils his uncontrolled desires. He is lawful but a covert tyrant cunningly making others grant his wishes. He is selfish, unconcerned with others' well being, a paradigm of a dharmically non-dharmic king. Such persons make willing slaves of others through moral pressure and get away without overt violence. India for half a century has been full of Yayatis.

Moksha through Social Service

Since the nineteenth century, there have been many streams of thought in India that made money making a sin. In ancient India, acquiring wealth (*artha*) was one of the four Hindu *purusharthas*, the four celebrated aims of human life. The wealthy man was supposed to earn fame by making donations and providing social support in various ways. '*Daana*' was a heroic act that the *vaishya*, lower in *varna* hierarchy than *kshatryia*, performed to excel the king to whom wealth came by the right of taxation and not by effort or *shrama* as in the case of the merchant. At the end of the Mughal sway, when India ceased to be a flourishing economy and the mercantile control gradually shifted into the British hands, European Orientalists and the Indian scholars alike created the image of India as a primarily spiritual culture that held the ideal of collecting wealth at a low priority. Enlightenment and liberation, *jnana* and *moksha*, were valorized as her primary civilizational ideals par excellence.

While medieval Hinduism had held the *mokhsa*-seeking ascetic to be the paragon of humanity, the 19th century Hindu revival began replacing the medieval ideal (partially to combat the Christian doctrine of divine love for man's redemption) through the *moksha*-seeking-ascetic who was not a recluse but a social servant. Vivekanand was the pioneer in this area, whose ideas were reiterated by Tilak, Gandhi and several others in their own ways for decades later. The upshot of all these theories was, money is meant not for personal enjoyment at all, but only for a social cause. It is not even meant for an aesthetic or celebrative ritual use, as these things, at this given juncture in Indian history are not important. The rich man, as Gandhi put it, was only a trustee and not the actual owner of wealth. This ideal put Indians under a tremendous pressure as it denied to them enjoyment of wealth and other worldly pleasures, which was an age-old legitimate *purushaartha*, called *kaama*. This new ideal of Gandhian austerity for public service was never internalized by Indians and never pursued with seriousness except by the confirmed Gandhians like Vinoba Bhave and some others.

But it dominated the intellectual discourse and the political ideals and created a schizophrenic social behavior. While it demanded that its leaders and role models to be serving in abnegation, the inner desire for acquiring the good things of life was understandably too strong to be resisted especially when it had a sanction in the Hindu tradition and a facilitator in modern technology. As the modern Indian political philosophers distorted the balance of the four aims of *dharma, artha, kaama* and *moksha* by keeping the medieval supremacy of attention on *moksha*, a culture of hypocrisy became the norm, which made Indians into Yayatis.

Strangely enough, the religious ideal of *moksha* through social service facilitated the great fascination of Indian intellectuals for Marxism. For some traditional thinkers, social *moksha* was a greater ideal than individual *moksha* and the Marxist emphasis on social change seemed attractive. Some also looked for a precedent for the social concern in Buddhism, which they thought, placed a higher premium on the liberation of others than was the case in Vedic faith, as it was Buddha's compassion that urged him to save others. Parallels were drawn between Buddhism and Christianity on this ground. Others argued that an equitable social order was a necessary precondition for spiritual uplift, while others rejected any kind of traditional Hindu approach and regarded dialectic materialism as panacea for Indian ills.

The eventual installation of Marxism in India came when Nehru took over the leadership of the nation at Gandhi's death. In a way it was Nehru's great fortune that Bose, Gandhi, Aurobindo (a great voice even though a recluse) and Patel, all left the scene so that he could use the sentiment of the *moksha* through social service for his Socialist State. This was an attitude which all of these men would have challenged for sure as they were not satisfied with mere elimination of social inequality but also valued the aims of spiritual quest. In their absence Nehru cashed on the momentum for self-abnegation and made it serve with obedience to the Socialist State. Ironically the new Socialism also provided a happier ground for Yayati-like satiation of worldly desires, as it did not require abnegation. This new materialism did not advocate asceticism; it wanted only an equitable distribution of goods. It was *moksha* not through social sacrifice but *moksha* through equal indulgence.

Corruption, the Crown Gift of the Socialist Raj

Further, under the Socialist State, it was no longer the job of the individual to help elimination of poverty or render social service through personal efforts like charity but of the State to do so by changing the structure of wealth distribution. Personal charity or '*dana*' in any case could not be practiced in the new state that looked upon personal wealth and property as a social evil remnant of the capitalist society. While the Gandhian man was permitted to keep wealth as a trustee of the poor and not enjoy it, the socialist citizen was not supposed to have any wealth at all. In any case, the country as a whole under state ownership of resources became poverty generative like other Socialist states of the world.

Nevertheless, the Socialist State in India brought plenty of wealth to those who directly or indirectly managed State governance. The Yayati who knew how to keep on the right side of socialist *dharma*, found a way to force others to satiate his desires. He had his legislative, bureaucratic, or boardroom position (Devayani) as well his bribe-income (Sharmishtha). It is true that minions of the state have always practiced a degree of corruption and even ancient political thinkers like Kautilya had advised monarchs to keep in check extortions ('*utkocha*') by officials. But in the command economy set up, bribe, commission, extortion and undeclared assets came to acquire the status of a parallel economy, illegal but socially admirable. It came under the socialist *dharma* just as Sharmishtha had come to Yayati under the '*daasee*' *dharma*.

Today there is no sphere of Indian life, concerned with the affairs of the State or otherwise, which is not affected by underhand influence. Whether it is marriage, admissions in schools, license for business, income tax dues, payment of electricity or revenue bills, a seat on the train, funding of political parties for elections or the choice of their contestants, all transactions are governed by illegal exchanges. Indians are divided into two clear modern *varnas,* white and black, the man who earns an honest income and one who has an illegal one as well.

From Yayatis to Kamsas

The illegal content of social transactions that first began as a minor influence has now increased to be a major one. Sections like underworld criminals, political musclemen, legislators under trial for heinous offences, kidnappers, extortionists, drug dealers, international arms dealers and terrorist groups have an increasing say in the daily governance of the Indian State and country's business transactions. *The parallel economy of black money is turning into black governance or governance by death.* A whole corridor running through the Indian territory from Nepal to Sri Lanka is feared to have been formed and controlled by terrorists, political subversionists and criminal gangs. Yayatis are being replaced by Kamsas.

For a decade, with some de-controlling of economy, contributions by rich non- resident Indians and the sale of cheap labour through information technology, there has been a brighter life for the urban middle class. But at the same time huge areas of rural territory are sinking into deplorable governance and daily violence against women, the poor and the weak. The moral duplicity that developed under a system of state controlled economy has now become a degradation that will not go away with the coming of any other kind of liberalized post-Socialist economy. Privatization of public assets and greater control of economy by the non-State sectors will make no difference unless a new ethics that abjures both undue profiteering and extortion is consciously promoted and achieved. Along with the new ethics must come the capacity to govern with discipline and justice without which no State can fulfill its duty to its people.

7

Disappearance of the Fourth Ashram

It is no small wonder that is *varna,* with thousands of its *jati* ramifications has stayed in full force in independent India but *ashram*, the second half in the twin concept of "*varna-aashrama*" *dharma*, has virtually disappeared. Biologically speaking, the ashramas as the four stages of life are universal, but their categorisation and the ordering of the activities (*ashrama-dharmas*) to be performed during them is an Indian cultural choice.

Everywhere in the world, usually the first two-three decades of life are spent in perfecting skills, the next two in achieving money and status, the fifth-sixth in getting pushed to the back rows and the seventh onwards in virtual retirement. But in India, within the scope of this universal trend, a strong non-consumerist agenda was deliberately built into no less than three of these four stages or *ashramas*. *Brahmacharya*, the first was a period for study and utter austerity; *Grihastha* though for earning wealth was also supposed to be of active charity; *Vaanaprastha*, was again meant to be for fringe or forest dwelling, for detaching oneself from family and town and, *Sanyaasa* for total inward looking and renunciation. Nobody can claim that these ideals were fully lived in the Indian past. They were lived as much as ideals are lived anywhere else in the world. Nonetheless they created a society which functioned differently from present day ones.

Obligatory Support to Art

As belief in the other world, *paraloka* and rebirth was strong, some activity to earn merit for future life was obligatory. For this charity, religious rituals and the pursuit of the arts were prescribed as undisputed methods.

Art was often called a "sacrifice" (*yajan*) which needed a little or no money. Besides spiritual merit, practise of and patronage to the arts provided refinement, subtle pleasure and a fair name. In societies, called "shame cultures" by anthropologists, where a sense of shame ("aidos" as in Homer or "*lokaranjana*" as in Bhavabhuti) compels individuals to strictly live up to social obligations. If art is spiritually meritorious (*shubham* or *mokshada*), pleasurable (*rasaanubhooti*) and a bringer of fame (*yashakari*), then it also becomes a major economic force and devotion to it becomes a social instinct. It is no exaggeration to surmise that it has been so in most periods of Indian history.

Enough proof of this is scattered all over the subcontinent in the great architectural and sculptural ruins of edifices that were raised not in one glorious period of a few hundred years, as was the case in Greece or Mesopotamia, but for two millennia. In an easy guess, one might say that India produced as much architecture and sculpture as rest of the world together. And it is also true that these extensive feats in stone were enlivened by a matching achievement in painting, poetry, song, dance and crafts which did not leave such unperishable traces. In other words, Indian society invested more heavily in the arts as a habit than most other cultures, and that too, not as an indulgence or escape but as a noble aim, as a worthy *purushaartha*.

Protestant Work Ethics

With the advent of modern technology in India also arrived very subtly an alien work ethics in which not to work for economic gain was considered as synonymous with parasitism. Every artistic preoccupation or deeper intellectual pursuit came to be regarded as a non-productive burden. Thanks to the Protestant Reformation in the West which denigrated art as panderer to baser insticts and the Christian iconology as a perversion of the true religion, puritanism travelled to India via Orientalism and became part of the so called Indian Renaissance. Leading figures like Dayanand Saraswati, Raja Ram Mohan Roy, Vivekanand and a host of others preached a puritanic lexicon based revival of tradition in which verbalisation was held in higher esteem than ritual practices and the dogmatic rhetoric hushed up artistic expression. That art can be emotionally elevating and hence contributive to the general health of society became questionable.

As a result even after half a century of Independence a poem or a song must demostrate its social utility, a *Bhairavi* or a *Desa* must lead to the national anthem, and holding classical music concerts must appear to be promoting national unity. Not only is the doctrine of art for art's sake or the theory of "*rasa asvaadana*" still an anathema, art for the sake of the sacred and spiritual is also suspect. It is viewed as a valorisation of priesthood and labled as "Brahminism" by our modern elite.

No wonder, we see that the US, richest nation and the trend-setter in the world, rushing at this moment to shed its welfare burden and art grants because the taxpayers (in ancient Indian vocabulary, the *grihastha-ashramin*) consider it non-obligatory to bear the burden of not only the artist, the thinker, and the non scientific researcher, but even of the sick, the old and the destitute.

By contrast, in pre-modern India, the *grihastha*s, or the house-holders, willingly and consciously bore the entire burden of not only the artist and the scholar, but also of the student, the recluse and the hermit, of all the people belonging to other three *ashrama*s. Obviously, an entirely different cultural psyche was in operation.

Making Room for Others

Social support to the *ashramas* of *Vaanaprastha* and *Sanyaasa*, in which people attempted to pursue learning and spirituality, not only provided a social space for these pursuits, it also provided an exodus from centre stage of social action. Like the power of mercy it was twice blessed, it blessed him that renounced and those that were renounced. Although one need not take the literary references of ancient kingly renunciations as reflective of the norm, in a pre-technologised society when demands on physical strength and fitness were much greater, succession, in any case, had to be effected much earlier. There is a similarity of situation with the modern sports people who retire at the first signs of their flagging prowess to avoid humiliation. The ancient hallow around renunciation, nevertheless, made giving up not only less difficult, but also irreversable. Besides, nobody then had the option of spending old age in infotained relaxation.

Modern Change in the Aims of *Sanyaasa*

In the four-fold classification of life pursuits, as *artha-dharma-kaama-moksha*, the aim of the fourth *ashrama* was total inwardness or self-realisation which may have been called by many names such as *nirvana*, *kaivalya*, *mukti* etc, but in no way any social action of a partisan nature was involved in it.

In the modern times, however, the Indian *sanyaasa* concept has undergone one major influence, i.e., the proselytizing Christian reformer. The Christian ideal of the monk as the healer, of the crusader in particular, was new to our subcontinent. Before that, Islamic proselytizing, whenever it did not operate under the sword, worked by offering proximity into an alternative cultural community, a different *millat* which was located at the lower rung of the ruling elite disbursing political power, economic benefits and some social mobility. The Christian convert in colonial times , however, could never be part of the ruling class even at the lowest rung, being colour barred, though he could benefit by moving into a somewhat healthier, better educated and urbanised Christian community. Hence the great Christian strategy of opening hospitals and educational institutions to widen their proselytizing impact.

To face the Christian challenge the Indian *sanyaasin* took a new role different from that of the earlier meditative wanderer giving casual advise to the laity. Like the Christian missionary he began working for development, social reform, revival and proselytization. Vivekanada was the first major saint who included many aspects of social reform in his spiritual agenda. Gandhi was the second great figure to combine spiritual quest with political and social change.

But in the absence of spiritual authenticity and discipline as practised by great figures, social reform was equated with political activism. The saffron robe soon fell at the mercy of blatantly commercial or partisan political activists. We have seen how NT Rama Rao, donned the ochre robes, ruled as the Chief Minister of a State and entered into a marraige in those very colours and how Uma Bharati serves as an MP working for the specific interest of a political party. The list of such political swamis is just too long. Who will believe that this kind of monkhood is dedicated to any sort of "*dharma-chakra-pravartana*", for inspiring better moral conduct and spiritual upliftment under a fresh philosophy. Equanimity (*samadrishti, samapravartana*), partylessness, and going beyond likes and dislikes (*veetaraaga*) have been the mental prerequisites for the fourth *ashrama*. Indian monkhood, on the contrary, is now being increasingly associated with social power and political pressure.

Lack of Credibility

The decline of *sanyaasa* as an *ashram* has largely resulted in the vulgarisation of hermitages. From centres of austerities (*tapobhumis*) they have becomes hubs of publicity (*prachaara-bhumis*) relying on clientele often political. The connection that obtains between the *ashramas* and political circles is notorious. Instead of purificatory spaces *ashramas* have become conspitorial.

The fourth *ashram*, thus, now stands in jeopardy. On the one hand its urge for social service is threatened by narrow political ends, on the other, social support for the intellectual and meditative monk (*muni*) is not forthcoming. With a few exceptions, hermitages or *sanyaasa-ashramas* all over the country are now full of less than mediocre preachers who aim to promote their mendicant organisations through wealthy disciples. One does not find in them, many *saadhakas* of *yoga* or other arts and philosophies. Surely the great tradition of Indian men in ochre robes writing great treatises and commentaries on philosophy, music, medicine or mathematics has virtually disappeared.

As there is not much thinking going on in the spaces of renunciation, there is little connection between them and the mundane centres of learning. The gap obtains not merely because of the differences between the traditional and the modern systems of education. Modern education and the Western systems of knowledge have been in India long enough. Enough *swamis* know English to hold discourses in it and travel abroad. But not enough doctors, engineers, scientists and administrators have taken to *sanyasa* or have held serious dialogue with *swamis*. And of course, hardly any politician of fame, except Vinoba Bhave, has taken the vows of the fourth *ashram* and retired for good. The contrast from the days of Buddha , Mahavira or even Chanakya (who never stayed to enjoy the fruits of power but went to the forest no sooner was his task accomplished) is a major cultural shift.

Is India a Senile Culture ?

When those who should have retired continue to wield power, the nation comes to live under the shadow of senility. We witness this in every sphere of our national life. Our artists, thinkers and scientists are repetitive, or at best Euro-intimidated; by and large, universities and schools have not restructured courses and their contents for half a century;

the bureaurcratic system has stayed perfectly colonial; religious, parochial and linguistic enclosures have tightened; caste barriers have been reaffirmed; caste endogamy is flourishing; every political party in India has arrived at an ideological dead-end as they have little more to offer than a tokenist jargon; the Congress still rants for fake secularism, the Left for caste struggle, the Lohia-Ambedkarites for job reservation, Muslims parties for Urdu and Personal Law and the BJP for objectification of Hindu culture. Freshness is not in the air.

Part Two

GRAMA : Dusty Villages, Dying Cities

8

Vote Bank Politics
Lame Duck Legislators

Having entered the twenty-first century India should remain under no illusion that legislative inactivism shall be the order of the day in our populist democracy. The root cause behind this inactivism is the populism practiced mindlessly by our legislators. To appease his prospective voters an average member of the Indian parliament, a state assembly legislator, a city corporation member, or even a village council (*graama panchaayat*) member, does not hesitate in making mutually contradictory concessions to different sections of his voters. He will promise raised fares to taxi associations and no increase in fares to the commuters at the same time. He will assure tax-cuts by reducing government expenditure, and at the same time promise to raise salaries and make fresh appointments in bureaucracy. He will show the lure of higher quality of education but in actual practice, flood the universities with excessive entrants and politicize student cadres. He will make new roads but jam them with encroachers and illegal constructions.

The list is unending. After a few decades of *placation without policy*, the contradictory pulls have brought an end to both development and governance. The frustrated public has turned to the courts for mandatory orders to be given to governments to sort out the mess. This awefull decline in the efficiency of the legislators has put them under the scrutiny of the judiciary and challenged their supremacy that had stayed uncontested under the socialist system practiced from Nehru and his dynasty. Several cliques of functionaries, dependants and parasites under socialist raj have bolstered the primacy of the legislators now in question.

It is also clear that the political elite have under their patronage vociferous apologists, that huge class of mediocrities who secure positions and favours which they cannot secure through fair means of promotion, and who continue to support the myth of the supremacy of the Parliamentarians.

Judiciary versus Legislature

After protests from politicians against some judicial announcements, and their attempt to ridicule the assertiveness of judiciary as "judicial activism", for some time politicians as a class had decided to lie low. The judiciary is winning popular appreciation of their role. The people of India, unlike her "committed" (read politically partisan) intellectuals, are quite sure that on major and minor issues alike, legislators of all levels are incapable of evolving a common agenda for solving basic problems.

It is not that the common man is expecting the Parliament to thrash out contentious issues complicated by years of politicking such as the dispute on the Ayodhya site of Ram Mandir/Babri Masjid, or the area and pace of economic reforms or the implementation of affirmative action along the caste lines. The Ayodhya tangle has already been entrusted to adjudication, and the issue of the creamy layer appropriating the benefits of reservation or affirmative action will have to be soon decided by the Courts too. It is not only bigger issues like taxing agricultural income, or updating rent laws, or a common civil code that the judiciary would have to adjudicate when matters are brought before it in the near future, but it is the small civic rights that will have to be clarified by the Courts and their implementation ordered. Now there is a total inability among legislators in taking and implementing policy decisions for running daily administration resulting in crisis after crisis which the judiciary has to diffuse.

Are Legislators Supreme?

Apologists for the legislators are never tired of pointing out that the Constitution has spelt the functions of the judiciary, the legislature and the executive very clearly and the lines demarcated for their territories are also well marked but in actual practice the legislators are getting increasingly impatient with the judiciary. They have launched several verbal attacks on the judiciary and one wonders if these are only a prolegomena to the day when hordes of party workers of all shades shall shout slogans in front of the Supreme Court against the judiciary of the land, a way they adopted to ruin the universities and business corporations in the heyday of socialism.

Now even the Prime Minister, Manmohan Singh and Speaker of the Lok Sabha, Somnath Chatterjee have advised the judiciary not to transgress their specified area and lamented their 'interference' into policy making by legislatures and rules of governance by the administrators. As the Press Trust of India reported through several newspapers on 8.4.07 in a public lecture there was a virtual debate between the Chief Justice of the Supreme Court and the Prime Minister. Justice Balakrishnan observed: "The application to judicial review to determine constitutionality of the legislation and to review the executive decision sometimes creates tension between the judge and the legislative and the executive branch. Such tension is natural and to some extent desirable." Noting that the judiciary's independence was essential to the rule of law, Balakrishnan said, "judicial review was an extraordinary legal invention that seems deceptively simple, but it is one of the most baffling of legal devices. Sometimes it is described mistakenly as a veto power over legislation."

In his retort the PM said, "The dividing line between the judicial activism and judicial overreach is a thin one . . . A takeover of the functions of another organ may, at times, become a case of over-reach." Like most members of his class he maintained "that the judiciary's primary obligation was to enforce the rule of law, uphold the Constitution and enforce the discharge of obligations by any authority of the state." In plain words, judges should be content with enforcing whatever laws the legislators make in their wisdom or lack thereof and not try to "substitute its power of mandamus to take-over the functions of another organ, meaning the legislature and executive."

And finally the stock argument came from the PM. The judiciary can deal with limited number of matters and has too much on hands already hence they should not try to review the decisions of the politicians and officials. "The courts do not possess a magic wand which they can wave to wipe out the huge pendency of cases, nor can they afford to ignore the instances of injustices and illegalities because of the huge arrears of cases already pending with them. If the courts start doing that, it would be endangering the credibility of the courts and the tremendous confidence they still enjoy from the common man." As if there is some body else to be blamed except the government for not appointing sufficient number of judges!

Of course, this debate was taking place at a time when several legislations had been struck down by the apex court, the latest being the constitutional validity of Schedule Nine and the stay granted on implementing the 27 per cent quota for OBCs in elite educational institutions. But there is more to it. The truth is that the legislators are feeling invaded.

The brief of the PM was further argued in a speech by the Speaker of the Lower House of the Indian Parliament, singing the same tune. While conceding the right of the judiciary to review laws he reiterated the platitude that they cannot frame them. "The framers of our Constitution took infinite care to provide for an independent and impartial judiciary as the interpreter of the Constitution and as the custodian of the rights of the citizens through the process of judicial review, which gives the mandate to the judiciary to interpret the laws but not to make them, nor to lay down general norms of behavior for the government or to decide upon public policy." (Excerpted from the Dr. Kailash Nath Katju Memorial Lecture on 'Separation of Powers Under the Constitution and Judicial Activism', New Delhi, April 26 reported Indian Express, April 28, 2007).

It is difficult to find a case where the judiciary has attempted to frame a law. If not, then why make this complaint? The judiciary has a constitutional right of striking down the laws framed by an unimaginative, partisan, and vote gathering legislative class. Doing so is exercising its powers of review. If politicians make bad laws that strangle citizen rights and if people ask for relief, the courts are obliged to review such Bills and Acts. Citizens cannot wait for a fresh general election to remove bad lawmakers. Besides the issue of a bad law is not to be decided at polls but at the level of those who understand the difference between public good and public pandering, between ethics and convenience, between *dharma* and *adharma*.

Politicians wish to continue in the vein of asserting political primacy. To quote again Shri Chatterjee who aired another platitude: "The Constitution does not contemplate a super-organ nor confers an over-riding authority on any one organ. No organ has any power to superintend over the exercise of powers and functions of another, unless the Constitution strictly so mandates." To buttress his opinion he mentions quotes earlier parliamentary debates and from Jawaharlal Nehru (whose rhetoric is too often given an undue aura of sanctity). "Intervening in the debate in the Constituent Assembly, many learned members had expressed the view that the doctrine of judicial independence was not to enable the judiciary to function as a kind of a 'super legislature' nor a 'super executive'. In the words of Pandit Jawaharlal Nehru, while speaking in the Constituent Assembly: "No Supreme Court and no judiciary can stand in judgment over the sovereign will of Parliament, representing the will of the entire community. If we go wrong here and there, it can be pointed out, but in the ultimate analysis, where the future of the community is concerned, no judiciary can come in the way . . . ultimately the fact remains that the legislature must be supreme and must not be interfered with by the court of law in measures of social reforms."

One must pause to think of the deep consequences of these statements. Firstly, these are words of Chatterjee and Nehru, not of the Indian Constitution nor do they carry its import accurately. Judges challenging the acts of politicians will always seem "super legislature" and "super executive" to politicians. But not to the people who feel wronged and look for relief. Secondly, these words of Nehru should not be used to preach an unconstitutional primacy or infallibility, let alone any 'supremacy' of the legislative class. Being elected by the people does not transfer any unalloyed wisdom on the legislators. On the contrary they are known to succumb to many influences often working against public good. One may read an old text like the *Arthashaastra* for the warnings to the monarch against temptations and subterfuges.

The temptations of modern psephotheria (vote-hunting) and global favors are much greater than in ancient days. Once elected, peoples' representatives may not keep, and in the past for many decades they have not kept, peoples' welfare and wishes in mind but may act in utter self-interest. Who shall check them if not the judiciary and a strong vocal intellectual class? The intellectuals have no constitutional authority, they can only talk, plead and publish but the courts can act and the Constitution clearly provides for that. The sooner our legislators and politicians shed the illusion of their supremacy, the easier will it be for the people to keep their faith in democracy. The right to make laws is not supremacy but a function to be discharged with humility. Moreover this function is open to questioning by the people who can ask the courts to review them. The Indian Constitution is not the manifesto of a Russian or a Chinese totalitarian Marxist state, which enshrines unlimited rights in the rulers under the garb of 'will of the proletariat.' Is India collapsing into a totalitarian system keeping the showy shell of democracy?

The politicians are disturbed by the recent orders of courts, which they consider an encroachment. In the Lok Sabha speaker's view, "courts have apparently, if not clearly, strayed into executive domain or in matters of policy... the orders passed by the hon'ble high court of Delhi in recent times dealt with subjects ranging from age and other criteria for nursery admissions, unauthorized schools, criteria for free seats in schools, supply of drinking water in schools, number of free beds in hospitals on public land, use and misuse of ambulances, requirements for establishing a world class burns ward in the hospital, the kind of air Delhiites breathe, begging in public, the use of sub-ways, the nature of buses we board, the legality of constructions in Delhi, identifying the buildings to be demolished, the size of speed-breakers on Delhi roads, auto-rickshaw over-charging, growing frequency of road accidents and enhancing of road fines."

The Speaker and all politicians obstinately choose to forget that the people were forced to rush to the courts as the legislators and administrators have failed to act as they have stayed under the pressures of the groups that resist change and wield money and vote power to perpetuate status quo. In fact, these two pillars of democracy have abandoned real social reform. Judiciary the third pillar is compelled to take the burden not out of choice, not out of judicial activism, but to fill in the dark chasm created by legislative and executive inactivism. All these issues were not taken suo motto by the judges but because the people went to knock at their courts. Should they have slept like the parliamentarians to wake up only to shout and squabble in the wells of the Parliament and Legislative Assemblies?

Unfortunately, in spite of severe erosion of daily governance and spreading mutinies, politicians are still in the Rangila syndrome of slothful self-enjoyment. Like the Muhammad Shah of yesterday, they still think that 'hunoz delhi door ast' (delhi is still too far) for the Nadir Shah of anarchy to arrive and capture the Indian State. They are not worried about what the courts do as they know that the courts are already working overtime and beyond a measure, they cannot take issues of public interest or of constitutional nature for timely relief. Actually, the politicians have abetted in the delay in courts, as all governments have silently conspired to keep the number of benches and courts too few. So have the executive class forced too many people to take the road to litigation, by their frequently arbitrary and insensitive decisions, making GOI the biggest litigant in the land.

Half Baked Bills and Acts

Vote banking compels our legislators to hastily bring in bills that are genetically defective. The usual method is to introduce bills at the instance of certain lobbies that are vocal in media and influential as a class seeking greater aggrandization of their own image. The reformist atmosphere for the enlargement of women rights, protection of children from abuse, minority protection and similar issues helps many groups, particularly the NGOs with foreign support and collaboration. The Anglophonic Indian liberal class, as a rule ignorant of the social realities on the ground, chips in with their support through press and lectures in fashionable centers of discussion. The long-term interest of the Indian people as a whole and the compulsions of orthodoxy enforced by lack of education (of any sort, traditional or modern) are ignored in formulating these laws. It is believed that a new rule (that transforms into '*dandaas*' in the hands of the local police) shall be enough for social compliance, where as the truth is that until a fresh vision has not been achieved through education and public awareness, compliance of the new laws remains an illusion and in actual practice ends up in open abuse of the new law.

The most disturbing thing about these so called bills for social reform is that they follow double standards and are conceived not along the same principles of liberty, equality and fraternity but are divided into two categories, one for the majority of Hindus and the other for the minorities of Muslims and Christians. For Hindus they aim to usher in some sort of a global modernity but for the minorities they are meant to give a fresh lease to regression and orthodoxy in the name of 'protection of minority rights'. Nehru initiated a number of reforms, modernizing and democratizing the Hindu marriage and inheritance laws. These reforms were also applicable to Sikhs, Buddhists and Jains (all three defined as Hindus by the Supreme Court for marriage laws). The reforms forbade Hindu men to take more than one wife, prohibited child-marriages, and gave daughters and sons equal inheritance rights. However, the Muslim community was exempted from these reforms.

The hype that follows the formation of these half-baked laws serves to falsely project certain members of Parliament, women activists, film actresses, peace-nicks and some retired bureaucrats as fore-runners of reform. These people are often decorated with Padma awards, UN recognition and finally fat sums of financial aid to the institutions these worthies patronize. To make their images super effulgent these self-seeking reformists make the laws as sweeping as possible often without appropriate checks and balances. Such bills that eventually get enshrined as Acts in the Constitution, impossible to amend in spite of the growing damage that some of them continue to cause. The list of such new laws is long but some of them may be mentioned to illustrate the fact that they have caused more regression than any progression that their formulators boasted about.

Shah Bano Case

The most prominent of these is the Muslim Women (Right to Protection on Divorce) Act, 1986, popularly known as the Shah Bano case, exempting Muslims from obligations to financially support ex-wives. It was enacted by the Congress government of Rajiv Gandhi who untiringly claimed to take India to the 21st century but in actuality, succumbed to the pressure of the ultra conservative Muslim clergy that have always insisted on an uncharitable version of Shariyat laws that severely curtail the freedom of Muslim women in joining the modern mainstream life.

The ruling given by the Supreme Court of India that paved a well-lit path for Muslim divorcee women by awarding the same benefits that were available to the majority Hindu women. Begum Shah Bano, a middle-aged Muslim woman from Madhya Pradesh, was divorced/given triple talaq by her husband, MA Khan after 43 years of marriage. She filed a petition in the state High Court that as an Indian citizen she was entitled to financial support from her former husband. This penurious Muslim woman claimed for maintenance from her husband under Section 125 of the Code of Criminal Procedure. The Supreme Court judges in 1985, held that the Muslim woman have a right to get maintenance from her husband under Section 125. They observed: "This appeal, arising out of an application filed by a divorced Muslim woman for maintenance under section 125 of the Code of Criminal Procedure, raises a straightforward issue which is of common interest not only to Muslim women, not only to women generally, but to all those who, aspiring to create an equal society of men and women, lure themselves into the belief that mankind has achieved a remarkable degree of progress in that direction. Under section 125 (1) (a), a person, who, having sufficient means, neglects or refuses to maintain his wife who is unable to maintain herself, can be asked by the Court to pay a monthly maintenance to her at a rate not exceeding five hundred rupees ...'wife' includes a divorced woman who has not remarried."

They pointed out whether the spouses are Hindus or Muslims, Christians or Parsis matter little, as section 125 is a part of the Code of Criminal Procedure, not of the civil laws, which define and govern the rights and obligations of the parties belonging to particular religions. This section was enacted to provide a quick relief to those who are unable to maintain themselves. It goes across the barriers of religion even though it does not supplant the personal law of the parties.

The Supreme Court also tried to interpret the holy Quran liberally by pointing out that the verse 241 for divorced women says that "Maintenance (should be provided) on a reasonable (scale). This is a duty on the righteous." They also rejected the hard-hearted plea of the All India Muslim Personal Law Board that in verse 241, the exhortation is to the more pious and not to all Muslims.

Angry voices were raised against the verdict, leading to demonstrations all over India. The orthodox stand was that Section 125 CrPC couldn't apply to Muslims. Accepting maintenance beyond the *iddat* period was *haraam* (illegitimate) under the Shariat as all relationship between a man and his wife would have ceased. *Iddat* is a three months period to ascertain whether the woman is pregnant or not and if with the child, only the child is entitled to support from the father. After the triple utterance the woman could be supported either by her relatives or the Wakf Board. Islam does not allow alimony beyond the period of *iddat*, said the clergy.

To appease the orthodox, the Rajiv Gandhi's government skirted the issue that a secular relief in addition to the personal law can be given to Muslim women even though divorce may be decided according to Muslim personal law. The Congress party succumbed to the clergy and brought in the Muslim Women's Act, 1986. Apart from performing a ritual lip service of opposition, the well-sung progressives of the Anglophonic class also submerged into silence and some of them even sang odes in praise of the Congress for upholding the sanctity of the shariyat. This was a classic case of hypocrisy of the 'progressives', who routinely hold that a 21st century outlook favoring departure from older laws permitting of polygamy or primogeniture, is mandatory for the Hindu majority of India, while a perpetuation of Islamic and Christian orthodoxy for the sake of bishops and imams (who are often willing agents in the vote hunting of political parties) is in the interest of Muslims and Christians as it 'protects' their minority rights. 'Progress' thus prescribes one direction for Hindus and another for minorities. Not only does it make a mockery of the very idea of progress, it also ghettoizes the minorities leading to their alienation and profiling in Indian society. The Shah Bano Act helped to perpetuate the social isolation of Muslim women and their utter submission to the unbudging and ever fossilizing clerics who now frequently issue fatwas regarding women over and above the law of land. This outcome of the Shah Bano amendment has not been adequately scrutinized in the intellectual circles or universities dissertations on minorities.

Section 498 A

A typical example of attempting to remove a social evil (in this case of dowry and cruelty to married women) by making an over-harsh law is the case of a special provision called Section 498A, which defines the offence of matrimonial cruelty. This was inserted into the Indian Penal Code by an amendment in 1983. Offenders can be imprisoned as well as fined under the section. The offence is non-bailable, non-compoundable and cognizable on a complaint made to the police by the victim or her relatives. The section defines the meaning of *cruelty* as follows: any willful conduct which is of a nature as is likely to drive the woman to commit suicide or to cause grave injury or danger to her life, limb, or health (whether physical or mental) of the woman; or b) harassment of the woman where such harassment is with a view to coercing her or any person related to her to meet any unlawful demand for any property or valuable security or is on account of failure by her or any person related to her to meet such demand."

Made with the best intentions the law has met with a strange fate. It has not been able to provide the sought relief to the real victims specially those who come from poor or rural sections but it has been brazenly abused in urban areas by unscrupulous women and their families with the help of shameless lawyers. Even in divorce cases matters filed on grounds of incompatibility, lawyers frequently, rather as a rule, suggest to their woman client to take recourse to this section to pressurize the husband to meet her demands sheepishly.

The report of the Malimath Committee, submitted in April 2003, while ostensibly discussing the reform of the Criminal Justice System, discusses the "heartless provisions" of section 498A. The Committee(16.4.4), depicts the situation where:

> "a less tolerant and impulsive woman may lodge an FIR even on a trivial act. The result is that the husband and his family may be immediately arrested and there may be a suspension or loss of job. The offence alleged being non-bailable, innocent persons languish in custody. There may be a claim for maintenance adding fuel to fire, especially if the husband cannot pay. Now the woman may change her mind and get into the mood to forget and forgive. The husband may also realize the mistakes committed and come forward to turn over a new leaf for a loving and cordial relationship. The woman may like to seek reconciliation. But this may not be possible due to the legal obstacles. Even if she wishes to make amends by withdrawing the

> complaint, she cannot do so as the offence is non-compoundable. The doors for returning to family life stand closed. She is thus left at the mercy of her natal family."

The Committee recommends that the section be made bailable and compoundable to provide space and time for reconciliation. The Committee rightly suggests that the amendment shall be good for women as they would be able to get better maintenance which is denied now as the husband often loses his job in the pendency of the cases.

After report of the Malimath Committee, the judgment of the Delhi High Court on 19 May 2003 in the case of Savitri Devi v. Ramesh Chand and others (104 [2003] *Delhi Law Times* 824) took up the issue of "misuse." The Hon'ble Justice J.D. Kapoor, who has also taken up the matter in his book, *Laws and Flaws in Marriage*: *How to Remain Happily Married,* Konark Publishers, Delhi: 2002, in his judgment discusses section 498A. He "feel(s) constrained to comment" upon it as it "hit[s] at the foundation of marriage itself and has not proved to be so good for the health of the society at large." For him, section 498A results in the social catastrophy of thousands of divorce cases, primarily due to arrest of members of the family and the consequent reduction attrition that closes the chances of salvaging the marriage. He notes that in the Indian system remarriage is not so easy and women lacking in economic independence become a burden over their parents and brothers. He also notes the misuse of the provisions of section 498A by women complainants and the police. He acutely observes that the police are "bad and unskilled masters" in whose "iron and heavy hands" the "ticklish and complex" issue of domestic disputes should not be left. Further, the "misuse" by women complainants is explained only as the "growing tendency" among women to rope in each and every relative in the complaint. He ends up concluding that these "provisions were though made (sic) with good intentions but the implementation has left a very bad taste and the move has been counter productive." He suggests that the Section 498A/ 406 IPC be made bailable, and necessarily compoundable.

A special leave petition was filed in the Supreme Court of India, Sushil Kumar Sharma Vs. Union of India (UOI) and Ors – Jul 19 2005, Citation: JT 2005 (6) SC 266, Case No: Writ Petition (C) No. 141 of 2005, Judgment: Jul 19 2005 in which the prayer was to declare Section 498A to be unconstitutional and ultra vires and in the alternative to formulate guidelines so that innocent persons are not victimized by unscrupulous persons making false accusations. Further prayer was made that whenever, any court comes to the conclusion that the allegations made regarding commission of offence under Section 498A IPC are unfounded, stringent action should be taken against person making the allegations.

The apex court, however, dismissed the petition, taking the view that the "principle appears to be well settled that if a statutory provision is otherwise intra-vires, constitutional and valid, mere possibility of abuse of power in a given case would not make it objectionable, ultra-vires or unconstitutional."

The judges, however, observed that "the object of the provision is prevention of the dowry menace. But as has been rightly contented by the petitioner many instances have come to light where the complaints are not bonafide and have been filed with oblique motive. In such cases acquittal of the accused does not in all cases wipe out the ignomy suffered during and prior to trial. Sometimes adverse media coverage adds to the misery. The question, therefore, is what remedial measures can be taken to prevent abuse of the well-intentioned provision. Merely because the provision is constitutional and intra vires, does not give a licence to unscrupulous persons to wreck personal vendetta or unleash harassment. It may, therefore, become necessary for the legislature to find out ways as how the makers of frivolous complaints or allegations can be appropriately dealt with. Till then the Courts have to take care of the situation within the existing framework. As noted above the object is to strike at the roots of dowry menace. But by misuse of the provision a new legal terrorism can be unleashed. The provision is intended to be used a shield and not an assassin's weapon."

In spite of all these deliberation, the lobbies of social rights and un-reviewed progress persist in their march for more strident laws. Far from reviewing the section 498A to prevent its misuse, there are reports that The National Commission for Women has sought harsher punishment coverage under the Anti Dowry Act on grounds that there have been reports of dowry harassment even after nearly three decades of being married. NCW also wants the life sentence to be raised from seven years to ten years to help ward off the evil of "dowry." This hankering for the easy way out smacks of the colonial attitude that our so called reformers have inherited.

Governance in Decline

It is now taken for granted that the governments cannot clear the roads of encroachers, or keep the chain-pullers out of fast speed trains, or remove *tonga*s and *rikshaw*s from big traffic roads. They cannot save parks from being destroyed by marraige parties, fill telephone cable digs in front of the houses for months, pick up garbage or clean drains or prevent morning squatters on fly-overs. The populist demands that drive the average Indian politician are viciously contradictory as they are based on very parochial interests and petty vote banks. When one member of Parliament proposes that a law be enacted to make small family an eligibility condition for membership of Parliament it is opposed by another who fears that lower class representations would be reduced by such a restriction. If stray cattle is sought to be removed from busy roads, all parties combine to subotage the move as it displeases their urban-village voters. So the Chief Minister of every State advises people not to feed plastic to cows but leaves cows on the road to eat that plus other garbage. Who can give back the civic rights to the citizens if not the Courts?

At the same time it would be naive to invest too much hope in the efficacy of the judicial system given the pressures and the challanges under which it is functioning. At the district level the judicial officers have to distance themselves from the ruling class and have to resist administrative and political influences, particularly so in the non metropolitan areas. At the level of High Courts and the Supreme Court there is excessive piling up of cases and the rule of 'justice delayed is justice denied' obtains. Given the extra burden of compensating for legislative lame-duckedness and executive inertness and frequent wickedness, the public expentancy of relief from the judicial intervention shall turn into sombre frustration. For the present judicial rebukes to the executive decisions or lack thereof, seem glamourous on our blaring televisions, but the future is omnious. Deflecting the judiciary through the covert means of rabble-rousing by legislators is quite clearly in the offing. The number of unscrupulous and criminally charged legislators is so large that instigated unrest to seek favourable judgements is likely to be used relentlessly.

There has been a history of the legislature making severe attempts to constrain the independence of the judiciary, especially under the rule of the Congress Party when Indira Gandhi had imposed the State of Emergency in India from June 25, 1975 to March 21, 1977 under Article 352 of the Constitution of India, effectively bestowing on herself the power to rule by decree, suspending elections and civil liberties. During this unfortunate eclipse of democracy she had promulgated the idea of 'committed judiciary', which was just another name for eulogizing judges who fell in line with the wishes of the ruling party. As a matter of fact the attack on the judiciary began in 1973 with the superseding of three judges in the appointment of the Chief Justice of India.

Soon after the formation of Bangladesh, when Indira Gandhi had phenomenal popularity for show but an insidious Soviet influence from within, the import of the concept of a submissive judiciary was hardly surprising. As stated by Mohan Kumaramangalam, a well known Soviet supporter in her government, "In appointing a person as Chief Justice, I think we have to take into consideration his basic outlook, his attitude to life, and his politics. We, as a government, have a duty to take the philosophy and outlook of a judge into account in coming to the conclusion whether he should or should not lead the Supreme Court at this time. This is our own prerogative which the Constitution has entrusted to us." One can clearly see that the legislative class can easily slide into the illusion of considering themselves as superior visionaries who can have the right to dictate to the judges. During the Emergency, this right was fully wielded in rewarding the submissive and punishing the non-compliant judges. Plans were also floated for the establishment of a superior council over the judges. After a short absence, when the Congress Government was back in power in 1980, intimidation of the judiciary was renewed which included a filing of a privilege motion against the then Chief Justice of India.

A Supreme Court judge is appointed by the President, after consultation with the Chief Justice of India or with such judges of the Supreme Court or High Courts as the President may deem necessary (Article 124). A High Court Judge is appointed by the President on due consultation with the Chief Justice of India, the Governor and the Chief Justice of the High Court (Article 217). But it does not take much imagination to see that very wide discretionary powers are conferred on the President in selecting judges. With a compliant President, another goal that legislators of all parties are brazenly seeking, this discretion comes to the government of the day. So, as the law stands, the appointments are very much in the hands of the legislators as the Chief Justice of India must be consulted, but need not be respected.

In the last two decades, a major instrument of influencing the independence of serving and about to retire judiciary is the appointment of retired judges as chairpersons of various Commissions and Enquiry Committees. The number of such bodies is now staggeringly large and hence almost a certain post-career option. For instance, the chairperson of the

National Human Rights Commission can only be a former Chief Justice of India.

It is even more disheartening to see that the corporate world, professionals and academics have failed to speak out loud and clear in favour of preserving judicial indepedence. In doing so, they could have ensured their own independence, so much under increasing attack from political quarters. Like the proverbial frog in the well who turns a blind eye to the prowling snake gobbling fellow creatures and is helpless when it is his turn, the Indian intellectuals are divided and submissive. We see lawyers falling prey to their union leaders and confronting judicial officers at the slightest pretext, teachers welcoming vice-chancellors and registrars from the army or beaurocracy for factional needs, and business houses outwitting each other in licence procurement instead of unitedly demanding deregulation for free trade.

Under-Qualified Rulers

The Constitution for the modern Republic of India was formed by men who were worthy freedom fighters but not administrators in the least. Most of them were raised on the ideals of Western Enlightenment that was too anthropomorphic and racially biased and the Romanticism that overrates human excellences and overlooks the vicious in humanity. True to the education system of their times they had no understanding of the principles of governance formulated in classical or traditional India and had scanty acquaintance with the same in Greek or Roman times. The Constitution they framed rested too heavily on British and American models and sought to excel both by further idealization. Whereas ancient societies ensured strong eligibility restrictions on rulers through class, education and family backgrounds, the Euro-model which presumed that 'all men are born equal' translated into 'all men are equally deserving' to rule. Other than a minimum age and a residential affiliation the Indian Constitution demands no educational, moral or financial eligibility for contesting an election to its various elected bodies from a village panchayat to the Parliament. In the fifties the only recognizable qualification for a candidate was whether he had been arrested by the British police as a 'freedom fighter' and jailed for some period. In plain language, those who had suffered, however, briefly, under British suppression were now to be rewarded by legislative positions. Needless to say that those who made their claim to have fought for freedom were very often imposters and hence a very inefficient and opportunistic class came to be installed as professional politicians. By the seventies and eighties it was infiltrated by muscle men and money makers who profited from the vast corruption that the Socialist economy perpetuated.

It is time to rethink on the basic qualifications of the legislator. The opportunity to become a ruler that democracy provides to its every citizen has to be counter balanced by a demonstrated eligibility of that citizen in his/her moral conduct, educational qualifications and financial honesty before that person is allowed to contest an election. Any lapse during office should warrant immediate recall.

Some vision of the future is necessary to provide for a minimum efficiency to keep the wheels of administration running and avert disasters, some decisions displeasing smaller vote-clusters are unavoidable. But unfortunately, not only are our legislators unwilling to face this fact, they have no patience to let the bigger results bring them wider support. By their training they are not capable of even identifying the major steps that can bring the greater good. Here we fall miserably far behind the better organized Western democracies to which we often flaunt our claim of being the largest republic on earth.

The Aggressive West

In better working democracies in the West the elite consisting of politicians, businessmen, experts and intellectuals that rules majority population has the good sense "to agree not to disagree" on certain basic methods of civic administration, national security and social control. It provides certain freedoms, even in excess, for all and sundry, such as those of sex, pornography and profiteering through consumerist sales. But it does not compromise on national unity and integrity of the country. For instance, the US can allow Khalistanis to preach dismemberment of India and even train terrorists on their soil, but it keeps the Quebec separatists in check as splitting of Canada would be a disaster too close to home. Even the fellow white country like France does not allow its radicals to supply arms to the Quebec separatists much as it might be pleased to see the demand for a French speaking nation take shape on the North American continent. Similarly, the USA, while pretending to fight Islamic terrorism globally keeps the protection of its own soil at highest priority. It bombs Afghanistan and then Iraq in retaliation to Islamic bombing of New York, now known cryptically as 9/11, ironically a number for emergency help in the USA. But it allows Pakistan an "ally in the war against terrorism" to send *jehaadis* into Kashmir, Chechnya and vicinity and cause immense bloodshed.

While freedom of assertion by the ethnic and religious groups has been encouraged on the East European (the classic example of erstwhile Yugoslavia), Asian or African soil, the same is either outright denied (as to American Native Indians) or throttled (as to the Spanish Basques or the Turkish Kurds) or craftily contained by strategies of Cultural Mosaic and the Salad Bowl programs within the USA.

The Western societies have agreed between themselves to put on leash sub-nationalism within the territory of the West and to unleash it on the soil of the Rest. It is on the might of such unwritten understanding that in the 90's Samuel P Huntington made the glorious declaration that the West shall be able to hold against all the onslaughts on its hegemony in the coming century. He came all the way to New Delhi to advise India to rely upon America as she is going to be a lonely Hindu country culturally isolated from other civilizations. Just first five years of the new century have proved him wrong. Inspite of all bravado, in the fight against *Jehadi* Islam, the Western confidence is flagging, its war strategies are sagging and trust in allies is shaken.

It is clear that Western diplomatic principle of divide and thus rule Asia and Africa can no longer bear any fruit. The greater interdependence among all nations for facing global catastrophies, be it militant Islam, mass migrations, insecurity of investment or pandemics like AIDS and Cancer, they all call for saving thy neighbour as thyself. As the Western nations have the experience of guarding self interest, they have to rise now to protect international interest for their own national well being.

The ruling elite in India unfortunately, has still to graduate to have the capacity of making a consensus on issues of basic national interest. For one thing it has no experience of sinking its differences for the sake of fighting an extended war, or for ifluencing others. It is still divided ideologically along the Cold War division of Command Economy Left and Free Trade Right even though such a divide has ended for Russia and China. What is worse, our leaders have totally localised the American concepts of ethnicity along caste lines. India is now functioning politically as multi-ethnic and multi-caste state retaining command economy. In other words, like the erstwhile USSR, it offers all the possibilities of breaking up into Khalistan, Gorkhaland, Azad Kashmir, Bodoland etc., coupled with insurmountable state inefficiency inflicted by its public sector and subsidization.

Sadly for humanity, even sobering hardships such as long wars or earthquakes do not ensure politcal maturity. Our neighbor Bangladesh has been reeling from one natural calamity to another for nearly two decades but the fight between fundamentalists and progressives seem to be going in the favor of the former. Populist compulsions are too much for the leaders to take hard decisions. To remind oneself of the golden days of the much remembered Greek democracy, after Perikles died in 425 BC, "power went to ranting democrats from the other backward classes, like Kleon the tanner, and Hyperbolos the lamp-seller, who unlike Perikles relied less on their intellect and more on popular likes and dislikes that made Athens lose the twenty-three year long Pelopennesian war. Mere popular demands are never enough to lead a democracy, and are certainly no substitute to a leader's vision." (Oxford Classical Dictionory, 1970).

9

Voting Young

Ensuring Legislative Immaturity

Whenever an all party meet on electoral reforms is held in New Delhi it does not take long to conclude that the minimum age for entering Lok Sabha and Vidhan Sabha should be lowered from 25 to 21 and for entering Rajya Sabha and Legislative Councils from 30 to 25. The strongest proponent of this is always the party not in power which argues that younger legislators must be brought into elected forums as the voting age has already been reduced to eighteen.

That this argument is disarmingly simple is demonstrated by the fact no party expresses a reservation let alone any opposition to the proposed change. Surely the proposal seems to them as made in total national interest and not just in the interest of democracy. Consensus here emerges with greater ease than it could on the nuclear tests. In other words, not just the ruling party but every political party hopes to add to youthfulness in legislative benches, a green revolution in Indian legislature. But whether these 21-25 year olds would be mature enough to shoulder an increasingly complex and stressful decision making responsibility is never the subject of any discussion.

A closer look at the scenario likely to emerge if the age limit is lowered only reveals disappointing prospects. Although the average age of the Indian parliamentarian needs to be lowered, a twenty-one year old MP would in all likely hood be a highly volatile creature rushing more to the well of the House than the library of the Parliament. His formal higher education cannot be more than preliminary. At best he would have a mere BA degree, not even a Master's or a higher diploma. How much of national history, formal law and cultural diversity of the land is he likely to know ? Perhaps legislators do not think that any of these things are prerequisites for them! Currently a legislator is supposed to be a demonstrator par excellence ; one who knows how to organize rallies, *bandh*s and traffic disruptions at party's behest. A *shakha*, or a youth wing office with elder sycophants is school enough for his political training. After all, this is the hang-over from our struggle for Independence when political work was all agitation and no governance. To oppose the British amounted to serving Bharat Mata. In the sixty years of self-rule the political parties have never understood that mere opposition is unproductive. An MP today needs to be a good thinker and a careful planner. How much of this can one be, when barely out of college?

There is no thinking on the minimum qualifications for the legislators in India. Now that politicians are talking so bold of amending the Constitution in a significant way, is it indiscreet to suggest that basic qualifications of MPs, MLAs and other elected "public servants" may also be laid down in the improved Constitution? If the humblest rank worker in a public office has to show some formal academic achievement, why should it not be so for those who shape our destiny as law makers of the land ? Should it not be essential for a legislator to be more than a graduate ? Can he process files, reports and discussions without the personal ability to verify what is told to him by officials? Can he communicate to his international counterparts the interests of this country ? The gulf that obtains at present between the politician who comes by the usual qualification of a rabble rouser and the bureaucracy that he gets to command and manipulate, is extremely detrimental to nation building. The formal levels of legislative education must be raised mandatorily. Why forget that formal education of the leaders during the Independence struggle was very high and compensated for the relative backwardness of the average political worker.

Legislative Ethics

To turn the tide of agitational mode in which nearly all legislators find their refuge and to usher fruitful social prosperity, it is essential before and during the legislative tenure that every public worker must demonstrate a life of high moral conduct. During the struggle against British occupation of India, it was an unwritten prerequisite followed by almost all the freedom fighters of eminence. Perhaps for this reason, when the Constitution of India was written, the makers took for granted that nobody other than a self sacrificer shall pursue a political career in Independent India. They, therefore did not deem it necessary to incorporate eligibility qualifications and rules of conduct for legislators to keep the corrupt, the unscrupulous and the megalomaniacs out of legislative offices. This Romanticist vision of the Constitution framers has allowed criminal history sheeters, debtors, under trials or those accused of heinous crimes, to not only sit in the Parliament and Legislature, but to frame national policies in their favour. The number of such legislators is much too large and they punch heavier than their weight. The upright honest legislator is an unbelievable rarity. The next reform in the Constitution has to lay down fresh water-tight articles that disqualify legislators for specifically stated moral lapses, both from contesting the elections and continuing in office.

Lessons from Classical Morality

There is a marked difference between the classical thought and the post Enlightenment ideas regarding moral conduct and punishment. In ancient systems punishment whether as Greek Nemesis or Hindu Karma were regarded not only as desirable but as inevitable. It was the Cosmic Law, Dike or *Rtam*. The Romantic insistence on freedom to reform is a double edge sword. Whereas it very often opens a door to new life, it also allows the unscrupulous to repeat their crimes with impunity. In the absense of a well defined code of conduct, the incorrigible take over. Indian political system now stands vitiated for this very reason. Ancient societies, like the tribal cultures, enforced moral conduct (*aacharana*) more through a strong sense of shame and less through the judicial agencies. Modern individualism has nurtured itself by pitting itself against social norms and hence very often it mistakes licence for creativity, disobedience for liberty and indulgence for innovation. The sense of shame or public indignation being too weak, punishment or reprimand can only be handed out by courts of law, which are flooded with petitions especially in India. In the last two decades the omniscience of mass media has eclipsed moral reprimand and justice by creating controversies and contradicting versions of facts on which the media thrives for its own existence. The world today is put into a farcial but grim scenario where the terrorist and freedom fighter become exchangeable or even indistinguishable. We must come out of this confusion by taking a lesson from classical ethics of well defined norms and unavoidable retribution.

As an example of how the sense of shame operated in public life in medieval times we may turn to the Uttaramerur Inscription, a document that illustrates how the elections to village committees were held in the 10th Century A.D in the village by this name in Chengalpattu district south of Chennai. The document is found in the Annual Report on Epigraphy, 1904. It was the order of King Parakesarivarman, who conquered Madurai, for forming the Annual Committee, Garden Committee, and Tank Committee from the thirty wards of the village. To quote from the royal order:

One who contests must have the following qualifications:

(a) He must own more than a quarter *veli* of tax-paying land;(b) He must live in a house built on his own site ;(c) His age must be below 70 and above 35; (d), The contestant must know the *Mantrabrahmana*, i.e., he must know it by teaching others (this was a village of Veda teaching Brahmins); (e) Even if one owns only one-eighth *veli* of land, he should have his name written on the pot-ticket to be put into the pot, in case he has learnt one Veda and one of the four *bhashyas* by explaining it to others. Among those possessing the foregoing qualifications: (f) Only such as are well conversant with business and are virtuous shall be taken and, (g) One who possesses honest earnings, whose mind is pure and who has not been on any of the committees for the last three years shall also be chosen.

Disqualifications:

(a) One who has been on any of the committees but has not submitted his accounts, and all his relations, specified below, shall not have their names written on the pot-tickets and put into the pot;(b) The sons of the younger and elder sisters of his mother, (c) The sons of his paternal aunt and maternal uncle, (d) The uterine brother of his mother, (e) The uterine brother of his father, (f) His uterine brother, (g) His father-in-law, (h) The uterine brother of his wife,

(I) The husband of his uterine sister, (j) The sons of his uterine sister, (k) The son-in-law who has married his daughter, (l) His father, (m) His son;(n) One against whom incest (*agamyagamana*) or the first four of the five great sins are recorded, (o) All his relations above specified shall not have their names written on the pot-tickets and put into the pot;

(p) One who is foolhardy; (q) One who has stolen the property of another; (r) One who has taken forbidden dishes (?) of any kind and who has become pure by performing expiation; (s) One who has committed sins and has become pure by performing expiatory ceremonies ; (t) One who is guilty of incest and has become pure by performing expiatory ceremonies. (u) All these thus specified shall not to the end of their lives have their names written on the pot-ticket to be put into the pot for any of the committees.

Mode of Election

Excluding all these, thus specified, names shall be written for pot-tickets in the thirty wards and each of the wards in these twelve streets of Uttaramerur shall prepare a separate covering ticket for each of the thirty wards bundled separately. These packets shall be put into a pot. When the pot-tickets have to be drawn, a full meeting of the Great Assembly, including the young and old members, shall be convened. All the temple priests (*Numbimar*) who happen to be in the village on that day, shall, without any exception whatever, be caused to be seated in the inı er hall, where the great assembly meets. In the midst of the temple priests one of them, who happens to be the eldest, shall stand up and lift that pot looking upwards so as to be seen by all people. One ward, i.e., the packet representing it, shall be taken out by any young boy standing close, who does not know what is inside, and shall be transferred to another empty pot and shaken. From this pot one ticket shall be drawn by the young boy and made over to the arbitrator (*madhyastha*). While taking charge of the ticket thus given to him, the arbitrator shall receive it on the palm of his hand with the five fingers open. He shall read out the name in the ticket thus received. The ticket read by him shall also be read out by all the priests present in the inner hall. The name thus read out shall be put down (and accepted). Similarly one man shall be chosen for each of the thirty wards.

Constitution of the Committee

Of the thirty men thus chosen, those who had previously been on the Garden committee and on the Tank committee, those who are advanced in learning, and those who are advanced in age shall be chosen for the Annual Committee. Of the rest, twelve shall be taken for the Garden committee and the remaining six shall form the Tank committee. These last two committees shall be chosen by showing the *Karai*.

Duration of the Committees

The great men of these three committees thus chosen for them shall hold office for full three hundred and sixty days and then retire.

Removal of Persons Found Guilty

When one who is on the committee is found guilty of any offence, he shall be removed at once: for appointing the committees after these have retired, the members of the Committee for Supervision of Justice in the twelve streets of Uttaramerur shall convene an assembly with the help of the Arbitrator. The committees shall be appointed by drawing pot-tickets according to this order of settlement.

Panchavara and Gold Committees

For the *Panchavara* committee and the Gold committee, names shall be written for pot-tickets in the thirty wards. Thirty packets with covering tickets shall be deposited in a pot and thirty pot-tickets shall be drawn as previously described. From these thirty tickets chosen, twenty-four shall be for the Gold committee and the remaining six for the *Panchavara* committee. When drawing pot-tickets for these two committees next year, the wards which have been already represented during the year in question on these committees shall be excluded and the reduction made from the remaining wards by drawing the *Karai*. One who has ridden on an ass and one who has committed forgery shall not have his name written on the pot-ticket to be put into the pot.

Qualification of the Accountant

Any Arbitrator who possesses honest earnings shall write the accounts of the village. No accountant shall be appointed to that office again before he submits his accounts for the period during which he was in office to the great men of the big committee and is declared to have been honest. The accounts that one has been writing, shall be submitted by the writer and no other accountant shall be chosen to close his accounts.

Present Day Value of the Uttaramerur Inscription

What are the possible lessons for today that can be drawn from this example even though this constitutional requirement may seem too elitist and harsh to us and that too for small things like managing the village irrigation, gardens and festivals? It seems that the essential spirit of this constitution rests upon some very sound universal ideas of democracy. Here the main presumption is clear that the individual and his family are much smaller than the village interest. The governing spirit of this document is in accordance with the line we quoted earlier, *graamaarthe kulam tyajet* (for the sake of the village give up the family interest). A very high standard of moral conduct in private life had to be exhibited before one could claim to stand for any public office. For this reason it is essential that the contestant be more than 35 years of age, as by that time, he shall have had the time to demonstrate his dharmic conduct of not pandering to selfish or family demands. Why a similar requirement cannot be imposed in modern times? Modern democracies are so naïve that they presume that a fresh legislator should have the freedom to show his honesty after assuming office and need not have a track record of it in private life.

The Uttaramerur contestant was also required to have sufficient personal income so that he did not make his office a road for removing his poverty. This very wisely imposed qualification may be unacceptable in modern times as enterance of the ordinary citizen to legislative bodies is considered some kind of a fetish in today's democratic thought. But if it is not so, we may be spared of so many legislators from very humble origins amassing unbelievable amounts of wealth. One may let this condition pass if the requirement of notable educational achievement made an essential prerequisite. The Indian Constitution really needs to lay down some substantial educational qualifications for legislators, as the world today demands many accomplishments from the legislators, especially after the process of intense globalization. Governance is too complex now to be understood by untrained minds.

Another notable qualification is that the candidate should not have served in office for the last three years. This condition prevents the perpetuation of one's social elevation and leaves room for other incumbents. Modern political institutions really need to frame guidelines for limiting the number of years one can serve in the State assemblies or Parliament. The limitation of two terms for the American president is a good modern example. The career politician who knows no other vocation except politics and thinks of a temporary withdrawal from political office (except as defeated contestant) as death of his career, is perhaps not so much of a dedicated being as a deadened being. Indian political scene for a more than a decade now has come to be crowded by senile and infirm leaders who refuse to vacate the space for more efficient and dynamic successors.

The Uttaramerur document may offend modern notions most by the disqualifications it imposes upon the contestants. If they failed to complete the assignments earlier in office or are guilty of a host of other moral lapses, they are simply debarred. Not only the offender but his extended family and close relatives are also debarred. This may seem too harsh and even unjust today as we have elevated individual rights to an excessive level and relegated community behaviour to very low standards. Thus a wife or father let alone a maternal uncle would not tolerate to be penalised for his relative's misconduct. Also, moral notions of freedom to repent and have a chance to start a new life after moral lapses seem to have also allowed a much higher degree of permissiveness and laxity in social conduct. And above all, judgement is inordinately delayed in modern societies whereas it came very quickly in pre-industrial societies.

In the Indian judicial system today delays are so great that they best illustrate the proverb, justice delayed is justice denied. The delays have contributed more than anything else to the plunging of moral standards to the abysm and unscrupulous politicians are foremost in taking advantage of the delays. In such a situation, there is no other way than barring from contesting and removing from office against whom any criminal charges are framed by a court of law. If this is the law today for government servants and other employees why should this not be extended to our members of parliament and other legislative bodies? At least, the politicians would begin to create a system, which delivers judgements quickly for their own sake. Today they are getting away with the status quo.

Ill Effects of Lowering Voter Age

There has been no evaluation at national level if the decision to reduce the voting age to 18 has been really helpful either to the political parties or democracy as a whole. Every party lives under the illusion that it has gained, but the facts are so easy to ascertain. In the cities, not just *mufassil* towns, the BJP may have gained a little more of the middle class 18-21 year old vote but it has very little control on its gains.

On the contrary the ill effects of lowering the age to 18 are well known. Any college teacher will tell you that political parties have intensified their activities on campuses and further vitiated the academic atmosphere. The criminalisation of higher education has multiplied many fold since Rajiv Gandhi ushered in this change. Instead of involving the young in the political process as opinion makers, it has alienated them from political activity which is totally monopolised by the criminal-political nexus. Those who remain politically active are divided along party lines. Now offering the possibility of MPship at 21, makes campus politics irresistably lucrative. In which other profession can you hit the jack-pot so soon? In a career with such high stakes there will be no holds barred. We do not have to wait to see campuses become dens of criminal excellence. They already are, as is seen from the various incidents all over the country.

Actually decisions of electoral reforms often reflect the sickly anxiety of the political class to usher in their wards and proteges. In an age when special music, clothes, or films can be manufactured and marketed for todlers and teenagers, projecting immature and ignorant candidates as representatives of nation's youth will not be a difficult strategy. That these young men and women shall serve their mentors blindly is not anybody's guess but the writing is on the wall. And if one third of the seats in legislature do get reserved for women, in the scuttle to find suitably docile candidates, not only wives but daughters may end up playing a greater role. A wife, after all, only imbibes political wisdom, but a daughter is born with it in her blood.

10

Caste Choudhary
The New Age Parasite

In the fifties, children had a *chacha* in Nehru, esteemed not only by their parents but internationally. There would have been nothing wrong intrinsically in this metaphor of kinship which projected the newly emerged nation as a well-knit family, if not for the fact that most of Nehru's "nephews", not only the *lallus* and *munnas*, but even the proteges of the anglicised upper class, the "baba log", did not grow out of the *chacha*-syndrome. Times were such that in the Socialist Permit Raj most Indians had to depend on godfathers rather than on efficiency and hard work to rise in life. Thus emerged a nepotistic India of crippled entrepreneurship and gutted self-confidence. But there was a redeeming feature in Nehru's *chachadom*, it was beyond caste and creed. Yes, it had some preferences, as for English over Hindi, for literature over music, for rhetoric over ritual, for breeding over boorishness, but its fairplay was not usually in doubt. In any case, nobody else wanted to be a *chacha* or a *tau* to children as they did not vote.

More Plebian the Better

It was soon discovered that it is more rewarding to play *chacha* or *tau* to grown ups than to children. Not only the medieval panchayat allegiance to the caste elder promises a vote bank to the politician, the populist sentiment also wants the leader to be from the masses. Did not Aristotle say that the tragic hero should have a character neither much above us nor much below us ? He should be like us. Thus began the era of political leadership with personalities close to the lowest common denominator of the population. Now the leader could simply set aside complicated rules and norms, cut through the Gordian knots of law (even if tied by the Supreme Court) by amending the Constitution and implement his will to the dazzlement of the populance. Paradoxically, feudal obsequiousness and modern populism combined to throw up men who could make a virtue of excellence-shortage. The seventies witnessed the rise of many leaders in North India who boasted of themselves as 'sons of the soil'. The phenomenon had another edition in the South. Instead of 'sons of the soil', they were idols of celluloid. But both were equally anti-elitist. They prided in their humble origins although caste-wise they hardly ever came from the lowest levels. In the North, they were middle caste land owners or 'chaudhary', usually Jat or Yadav, and projected an authoritarian charisma in the style of the village headman. Charan Singh, Bansi Lal, Devi Lal of Haryana, Karpuri Thakur and later Lalu of Bihar and Mulayam Singh of U.P. all stand in this gallery. In the South NT Rama Rao, MGM, Karunanidhi and others depended again on the landowning castes.

The credit of displacing the accomplished lawyer, scholar, or a self denying social worker from the ranks of political leadership and replacing him by the strongman backed by muscle power and hired hoardes of agitators, goes to Indira

Gandhi who formed the Youth Congress to support herself and intimidate the elderly Congressmen. This trend was taken up by all other political parties and so was born the culture of roughshod politician who valorises brawn over brain.

Caste Chaudhry Always Parochial

With the rise of regionalism, fanned by the formation of linguistically demarcated states, the Government at the Centre became a target as if it was the sucessor of the Imperial rulers. Indian provinces, or their parts, have been always harbouring subnational feelings, which have sometimes turned into separatist demands. But it was with the coming of Mandalsim when regionalsim further split into the caste-vote banks, that the rabble rousing caste-chaudhry began his field day.

In the pre-industrial days caste identity was supported by transmission of skills within the extended family thus giving an economic demarcation to caste. In the medieval period institutions of higher learning, scholars, artists and artisans could not be supported by patronage of the State. Thus developed sub groups of caste-within-caste within which alone could lodging, touching, cooking, eating, travelling be undertaken. The creation of narrow subcastes within a bigger caste and their hierarchy was undoubtedly the product of an insecure society. Except for a short time during the Mughal rule, invasions and interregion wars were so many that social interaction at a larger national scale was drastically reduced. Migrations of population for trade, services and artistic performance was rendered minimal. But what was seen in abundance was displacement of communities and populations fleeing their homes at a large scale from the twelfth century onwards till the British rule. When people get displaced, they form ghettos in their new homes. Even when prosperity returns the mind remains ghettoised. The severe caste endogamy, taboos on food, clothing and conduct and most of all, severe restrictions on the education and the freedom of women are products of a society living under seige. With the coming of modern technologies of rail, print, bus and development of common public spaces like hotels, restaurants, schools, colleges and offices, most of the taboos began to vanish except for endogamic marraige or the *roti-beti* relationship which too would have gone with the breaking of the larger joint family, but for the electioneering on caste grounds which gave it a new *raison d'etre.*

The consequences are there for all to see. Regional caste is the determining factor for legislative choices today. So much so that a Mulayam Singh Yadav, Laloo Prasad, Vaghela, Badal, Jayalalitha, Mamata or Mayavati are hotly wooed by CPI (M), Congress or BJP, their veneer of national status notwithstanding. The politics of alignment may have endless rhetoric or umpteen slogans, but down below it is a game of musical chairs based on caste hatred where the foe of your enemy is your friend. And so the two Yadavs cannot unite, not even for their caste, let alone for standing up to the upper castes, nor can a Mayavati befriend a Mulayam. The caste-Chaudhary, thus fails to be an all India leader. His strength begins and ends with the home state and his caste. A person from the South belonging to the middle level land tilling caste say a *Vanyar* or a *Kamma*, cannnot identify with a Lalu Prasad or Mulayam.

There are many in India who believe that caste-chaudharism is "deepening of democray", an "assertion of federalism", and a "balancing of discordant strains within the nation symphony." So do the propounders of regional-caste-ethnic identities who preach that the creation of the other is essential for the creaton of the self. This conflict based philosophy for the sustenance of identities is surviving, and is being nurtured, mostly in the Third World and not in the first world as we shall explain in a later chapter, 'What is Ethnic'.

On the Indian Scene, ethnicity and parochial diversity cannot be used to demand exclusive attention or compensatory concession. The transformation that is brought about by the new technologies pushes the people of this nation into greater mobility and resettlemet across the nation and beyond. Indentities of the caste and region are melting very fast and forging into broader and more inclusive categories. 'Karachi halwa' is no longer made in Karachi only nor *idli, dosai* in Tamil Nadu. It is all Indian cuisine. The caste-chaudhary politician is failing at the national and most so at the global level.

11

Caste Endogamy
A Return to Medievalism

Princess Diya Kumari of Jaipur in the 90's had her way to live happily hereafter with the man she loved like the heroine of a blockbuster film but things have a gruesome end for those who so dare to marry for romance in India's villages. Not long ago were two young lovers slaughtered by their own parents in a UP village as the they were regarded as "brother and sister" (*sagotra*) being of the same village. In the confines of the capital, it is customary to flout the caste restrictions for marraige. A Rajiv can marry a Sonia, an Indira a Firoz, for such has been the way of the ruling class right back to Chandragupt who wed the daughter of the Greek *mleccha* Selefkos. But for the ordinary folks there is a different set of rules, which has remained the same in democracy as it was in monarchy.

The prevailing casteism in electoral politics ripping the nation apart is not a sudden upsurge. It has nearly half a century of growth nurtured by our national heroes and by each and every major political party. Since Independence, there has been a virtual acceptence in India of the Western interpretation of Indian culture as a *jati*-ethnic society consisting of regional and religious groups with little underneath their life styles which could be called a common and intransmutable denominator. What is worse, besides the political leaders a large section of our intellectuals have accepted the categories of ethnicity as defined by Western politico-anthropological establishment and applied it for social engineering in India.

Gandhi was a staunch reiterator of the caste (*chaturvarna*) system. His vision did not extend to the supplimentary *ashram* concept (the four stages of life), otherwise he would not have prescribed *brahmacharya* to householders and made "little men out of women" as Raja Rao put it. To suit his doctrine of *ahimsa*, he could go to the extend of explaining Kurukshetra not as the site of physical conflict but a metaphoric battlefield depicting the agon between right and wrong. For the caste system, he never said that all societies are metaphorically divided into intellectual, ruling, trading and service groups, and the four *varnas* today should mean nothing more than that. Instead he insisted that Indians observe in marraige alliances all the traditional *jati* barriers. Gandhi never encouaged intercaste marraiges, far from giving a program for them. He wanted untouchability to go but not the concept of hierarchical purity on which the *varnas* and *jatis* are based. Hence his Harijan uplifment remained superficial.

Ambedkar, like many others, was a victim of those European theologians, historians and anthropologists who falsely propogated that *varna-jaati* was a Hindu theological structure and Buddhism like Islam and Christianity had discarded it. Hence like a prophet, he believed, he led his people across the desert of Hinduism into the Buddhist oasis. Half a century has demonstrated that he was wrong, that *varna* is not a religious but a socio-economic division that all indigenous people have accepted throughout Indian history till the the ideals of liberty, equality and fraternity reached India. Caste does not disappear with conversion, if it could, there would be no demand by converts from Hinduism to non-Hindu folds to give them reservations.

Socialism Failed to Remove Caste

Nehruvian secularism, though it denounced caste in principal, had no reformist agenda. On the contrary, because it relied most of all in perpetuating orthdoxy and rigidity among minorities in the name of protecting their identities, it ended up giving a free hand to Hindu orthodoxy and regression. In the secular phase of Indira Gandhi's rule particularly godmen, astrologers, *yagniks* and *tantrics* haunted heavily the corridors of power and caste began to be translated into predictible vote banks. Western anthropologists conducted extensive studies at this time into the caste situation mostly redefining it as the sustaining feature of Hindu society. Secularism, thus, while professing to be progressive under the socialist umbrella, only served the cause of orthodoxy and hierarchichal reification.

With the fall of socialism at the global level and the introduction of the idea that in India, caste is class, by the Marxists, caste identities came into full play. They defocussed not only nationalism but cultural regionalism as well. The rise of the middle castes which garnered the maximum benefits of rural development, demanded a stronger participation in urban centres of power and succeeded in getting the adoption of the Mandal report. Here, the socialists and leftists also found a new cause to espouse and their dream of unity of workers and class struggle was replaced by the hopes of uniting the middle and lower castes plus minorities against the upper castes. The divide between the *savarna* and *asavarna*, thus, was made complete and is now the determining factor in Indian politics.

An attempt was made to contain caste divisiveness by Hindutva unity but as the means employed for it were tokenist and rhetorical, it failed. Socialism and secularism thus resulted in reifying the perfectly medieval caste stratification of India without its traditional aims of other-worldliness. Now there is a full scale entrenchment of caste hierarchies with different castes (minorities being *jatis* of another kind) competing for consumer goods. History offers many examples of such transformation. For instance, the Greco-Roman social hierarchy gave up the Olympian religion and reasserted itself through adopting Christianity.

Every political outfit, the largest two, Congress and the BJP in particular, wishes to keep the caste divisions. There was a hardly noted but extremely significant event of the Delhi Government taking back its scheme to promote inter-caste marriages on a near unanimous demand by legislators. Not only were the *savarnas* paranoid of exogamy, not one *asvarna* member of the House rasied his voice for the scheme. Protest from both Congress and BJP members alike against the intercaste marriage encouragement scheme came on the ground that "Marriage is a personal matter and Government should not interfere: it would disrupt the existing social order" (TOI, p3, 18.3.97). Obviously, the secularists and the Hinduists, were following the administrative lines of colonial predecessors. What greater proof that casteism fattens politcians!

The much drummed up difference between "secular" and "communal" forces has proved to be without substance.

The Congress, reduced to a *savarna*-base wishes to keep the rival *savarna*-based BJP out of power by enticing back to its fold the minorities, middle castes and the ST-SCs. The BJP, is trying to widen its reach by wooing middle and lower castes. It has been working hard among the tribals and forest dwellers to include them in the wider Hindu fold. Hence, it fights tooth and nail any attempt by the Christian and Muslim proselytisers to convert the tribals as once they convert to Christianity they shall be lost to the Congress, the party that has wooed the minorities at any cost even if it means the loss of national territory as in the case of Nagaland and Mizoram where the Christianised tribes are asking for secession from India.

The needling question remains, where does the nation go from here? Caste strife is not likely to abate as mechanisms to promote equality and fraternity are weakening. Urbanisation and mobility from the soil of birth has ushered in the gradual break up of the joint family which was the cementing factor behind caste endogamy. Given this scenario one expected that caste would have lost its grip. But the caste vote banking pushed by political engineering did not allow this to happen. At present no party has the courage to frontally attack casteism just as none talks of birth control since Sanjay Gandhi's misadventures. The challenges of the 21 century are too complicated to be met by a caste-ridden regressive society. In the coming decade, a divided India with its medieval social structure will have a poor bargaining power against a stronger East Asia and the very powerful West. It seems that after 60 years of independence the road to a covert subjugation of the nation has opened wide. Are we not the largest but also the cocksurest democracy of the world?

12

Politics of Compensation
Mandal, Mandir and Stri-mandal

Reservation or affirmative action, the Ram Janmabhumi –Ayodhya Mandir conflict and reservation for women to one-third of the seats in the Lok Sabha, have all one thing in common. They are based on the idea of "compensatory discrimination". For several decades Indian socio-political life has been rocked by "compensatory discrimination" through reservation of one kind or another. On closer scrutiny, it is found that this concept is one in the chain of Romantic ideologies churned out in the aftermath of Hegelianism. Like Marxism, Nazism, Zionism and many such ideologies, through a biased analysis of history, it chooses to set right certain wrongs and compensate the perceived sufferers for their deprivation through the ages. It is radically different from Christian and Islamic charity or Asian compassion that seek to help any sufferer or downtrodden and have no yardstick to make some sufferers more deserving than others. The results of Mandal and Mandir are there to see, it is worth investigating if "Stri-mandal" can go another way.

The Mandal Outcome

At the time when Socialist systems were collapsing elsewhere in the world and India too was faced with the challenge of leaving its Socialist cocoon, the change was resisted by reviving the Mandal Commission Report. The professed aim was to promise jobs in the public sector to a sizable number of people along caste lines which were defined as the Other Backward Castes (OBCs). These were regarded as above the Schedule Castes (*asavarnas*) but below the forward castes, namely Brahmins, *Thakur*s and *Bania*s or the *Savarna*s. There is an attempt to force private sector to follow suit. But as the private sector cannot forgo efficiency and accountability, the State alone has to provide reservations. For this reason, the public sector is still being protected in size and employability to retain "command economy" under a different name. Instead of socialism, we have now "social justice", the disastrous results of which are beginning to emerge.

Reservation for Vote Banking

Unfortunately, the spirit behind the upliftment of the socially and economically depressed has been perverted by our legislators. The system has been designed to create a creamy layer within every caste that shall act as the salesman of upliftment and broker votes for political power. That is why no criteria of low income is acceptable to our legislators for reservation for OBC or ST/SC. We see the ridiculous spectacle that the son of a ST/SC bureaucrat or judge or professor also gets the benefit and elbows out easily his poor fellow castemen. He gets all the benefits and concessions in admission to schools and universities, in eligibility for jobs, promotion in jobs that his truly deprived caste brother should get before he does. This flouting of natural justice and consequent denial to the actually disadvantaged poor in ST/SC/OBC, has been willfully perpetuated by the political class to augment the numbers of covert henchmen among government servants. If the aim was indeed upliftment of the depressed castes the propounders of 'social justice' would have long ago set some economic marker for those eligible for reservation and not left it to the courts to impose such eligibility. The aim, too blatantly, is to create power broker families along caste lines. The legislative class as mentioned earlier has decided to create newer and newer categories of people who are being newly defined as 'minorities' or 'deprived' so that the carrot of reservation can be dangled before them. The Congress is out to declare Jains as minority and extend reservation benefits to Muslims. Once this *lakshmana rekha* is smashed divisiveness in Indian society shall be unlimited.

After the Jains, the Buddhists, Ram-Krishna followers, the Vaishnavas, Shaivas and Shaktas all can claim to be non-Hindus and thus minorities and when within a decade Hindu fold splits a few dozen minorities, the whole edifice of majority-minority syndrome shall collapse making a mockery of the very concept of majority-minority distinction enshrined in the Indian Constitution. As a matter of fact, things have already reached a farcical level, though tragic, for the discerning.

While it has created bad blood on how much reservation is to be given to whom, it has also prevented the nation from progressing towards market economy by postponing infrastructural changes and rebuffing foreign investment. Moreover, it has not delivered the promised gains of the uplifting the people of reserved caste category either.

A Borrowed Model

Reservation as "compensatory discrimination" does not seek to eliminate the caste system, it merely aims to uplift some downtrodden castes, whether at the bottom or the middle of the caste ladder. Moreover, theorists of reservation are not clear about the manner of upliftment. They have borrowed the model of "affirmative action" from societies which do not have any rigid caste based hierarchy of *jati* (endogamic family) and *varna* (class based on purity level) as ours but only classes created by economic disparity. In such societies, now as always, economic advancement of a person, family or group, brings about a confirmed position into a higher class. But in the Indian system, prosperity alone has never upgraded the status of a caste (*jati*) into a higher *varna*. Upward mobility into higher class (*varna*) has been a complex phenomenon which comes after a few generations of struggle by a particular *jati* which also has to acquire the behaviour patterns of the next higher *varna* in food, social and ritual habits. Nevertheless, upward mobility has occured throughout the ages as one can make out from ethical codes, literature and ample researches of modern sociologists.

The present day reseveration policy, however, cannot provide upward caste mobility to a *jati*, though it may provide economic prosperity to some of its individuals. The beneficiaries have now a greater interest in sticking to their "down-trodden" *jati* label to ensure further financial benefits. No advantage now in a tiller (*bhumihaar*) revealing himself as a *kshatriya* as did Shivaji at his coronation. Now, instead of claiming closeness to Manu, or the line of Sun or Moon (*surya* or *chandra vansha*), it is better to be their victim.

(Reflected in an extreme case of a woman in Kerala claiming that her son was not born of her brahmin husband but from a SC rapist). The "uplifted" person thus lives in a schizophrenic state, part of him wishes to move up into the higher *varna* and yet another part preserves his caste certificate. Reservation, thus, has not only reinforced the caste system and embittered caste hierarchical interactions, it has created new perversions. Above all, not only the forward castes, but even the majority of OBCs and ST/SCs feel cheated as the benefits of reservation are gobbled up by the creamy layer of each category. Yadavs make hay, while Telis sulk.

The Mandir Aftermath

A similar "compensatory discrimination" for the Hindus by reclaiming the sacred sites of their famous temples from the "structures" or mosques built on their ruins, was at the root of "Ram Janmabhoomi" movement. The whole endeavour was steeped in cultural self-pity and lacked the ability to place Indian events in world history. Iconoclasm has taken its toll not only in India but in many places in the world. In Greece, the Christians erected churches on nearly all the sacred sites of Olympian religion from temple rubble.

The BJP and its politically sister organizations, going by the name of Sangh Parivar, had never thought that the movement would find so much favour both with the common and the intellectual Hindu. They merely went along with the rising tide and ended up with a massive electoral success, an undeserved windfall that gave them six years of ruler-ship in the Centre. Although, the Sangh Parivar had stated the concept of compensation for the Hindus from the Muslim community consisted of handing over three major temple sites of Rama Janmabhoomi in Ayodhya, the Kashi temple and the Krishna Janmabhoomi in Mathura by removing the mosques that were made over these temple sites by Babar and Aurangzeb, the Sangh did not prepare an extensive critique of Islamic iconoclasm and its pronounced hatred for the Hindu method of worshipping God through the icons (*moortis*). The demand was given a mere political shape, that is, compensation to the Hindus for the wrongs done to their temples in the past. But they did not take issues with the root cause, iconoclasm.

It should be obvious that the real aim of opening a dialogue with the Muslim world cannot be mere compensation but a pressure on the fundamentalist schools of Islam to recognize that in a pluralist world, idol-worship is a legitimate and a beautiful way of prayer that needs to be respected. This entails a major reformation in the psychological attitude of Islam towards Hinduism. A sustained dialogue with the Islamic clergy and leadership, through various means and at diverse levels, that is in social, religious, educational arenas, is required. The Sangh Parivar, unfortunately, did not, and still has not, taken up the challenge. They looked upon the Ram Janmabhoomi movement as a mere political ladder to leap into power. They once cashed it, then dumped the issue, not just as of reclaiming the sites, but also of persuading the Islamic clergy to restate their thinking on iconoclasm.

Other than a critique of Islamic thought as hostile to Hindu worship, as a corollary to the Ram Janmabhoomi movement, a major movement for the reform of management of the Hindu temples themselves should have been started by the Sangh Parivar and by all those who have the Hindu interest at heart. The Hindu temples, in general, have ill-qualified and often under paid priests. Graduates and students with even higher degrees from the many Sanskrit colleges of the country should be attracted to take up this vocation for their own welfare and that of the Hindu community. The majority of Hindu temples are supervised by sundry social groups that come from trader communities and lack the educational training that is required to operate such sensitive organizations. They are unable to utilize the donations that profusely flow in for cultural and educational purposes. Other than for some traditional kathaas and melaas funds are diverted to the wrong channels that now border on show business and even political placation. Thousands of grand temple complexes and holy shrines like Tirupati symbolizing the glory of Hindu architecture and cultural refinement have been taken over by the State Governments. Their massive donational income flows go into the public exchequer of the state and is not available to religious and cultural uplift of the Hindus. The armies of gazetted officers that are appointed to supervise these state managed Hindu temples, are a parasitical burden on Hindu pockets and are often the least qualified to hold such positions.

The many other shrines like the Vaishno Devi, that are very high in the estimate of the Hindu devotees are also taken over by the State Governments or holy sites like Brindavan are still managed by *pujaris* who have mostly abandoned the tradition bound life style of devotion to the deity and simply gobbling the temple donations as a matter of unchallenged right.

The Nehruvian syndrome of neglecting temples as the

age-old centers of learning and the arts, and instead privileging in the public mind, the dams and factories as the 'temples of modern India,' created an imbalance between the heritage and modernity. That temples can be revived and used as educational centres was beyond Nehru's vision and much more so beyond the vision of other Marxism dominated parties that held the Hindu temples to be irredeemable bastions of orthodoxy. The BJP also has never thought of the temple heritage in any serious way. Its claims of valorizing culture are tokenist and hollow. If the Ram janmabhoomi agitation had been made part of the larger effort of revitalizing Hindu temple complexes across the land, the result would have been spectacular and ever growing. Under the wider umbrella of a reformed and updated temple spaces for the modern and forward looking Hindu, the case for compensation of the three sites would have been stronger and more legitimate.

For the destructions suffered for several centuries, the compensation for the present day Hindus can only be, revitalization of the sacred sites into broadminded and all-embracing culture which brings freedom from fear of religious fanaticism of all kinds, including their own.

The Janmabhoomi agitation also diverted attention from the religious and cultural activity at local temples by focussing attention to a site far away from home. Collection of funds for the Janmabhoomi by the Sangh Parivar was also to, say the least, a dubious affair. Described by many as a counterblast to divisive Mandalism, the movement did not revitalise the Hindu community by breaking barriers of caste and orthodoxy. If it compensated anybody, it was the leadership.

Hopes from Stri-mandal

While Mandir is already on the back-burner of the BJP and Mandal a cause for despair, fervour for reservation has found new pastures: one-third seats for women in the Lok Sabha. Here the issue is seen not merely as India specific, but as the global problem of gender inequality. Hence credence is being sought for very vague, romantic notions such as ; men are showing a decline in initiative as much as in their sperm-count; women as leaders are more solution-oriented and less agonistic; as leaders they shall order fewer wars, and so forth. On the other hand, criticism of this reservation has aired fears of the Parliament becoming a Dolls' House, a coterie of arm-chair seminarians , an upper caste beauty saloon and the rest. But while most of these dangers cannot but be shortlived, what may abide can be the same as in the case of Mandal and Mandir, namely the entrenchment in power of a creamy leadership.

This feminine cream can be of all sorts, the jet-set seminarian funded by dubious NGOs or film lobbies, the lovely dancer husbanded by a diplomat, the OBC *sanyasini* who merrily and *chamatkarily* rolls tantric mumbo-jumbo with rights of the lower castes, the SC sister hopping from one political alliance to another, the minority "*motarmaa*" who proposes reform, freedom and light but in purdah. All of them the same, super-sisters, controlling electorate in the traditonal mother-in-law style. That the desire to dominate is weaker in women than in men, is anybody's wager. Just as mothers-in-law assist bride-burning and reinforce patriarchy, where is the hope that these women legislators will not look for their pounds of flesh perpetuating the status quo.

Feminine reservation in legislature has no meaning without an agenda free from political ideologies. Can the sisterhood pledge to materialize their agenda by disregarding male dominated party whips? Very doubtful. Only independent women candidates, can pursue the feminine welfare more freely. Their agenda can best evolve from a national discussion on elimination of glaring evils like forced prostitution, excessive child-bearing, wife-beating, dowry, purdah, female infanticide, caste barriers and molestations. To implement the agenda and change the social fabric should be the priority of women parliamentarians and not to demand more jobs for women or to promote the ideologies of the parties they come from.

This means a protracted battle against male politicians and a conflict with party hegemony in interpreting feminine issues and strategies. Political parties shall always try to derail the feminine agenda by making women legisltures serve the electoral agendas. The Mandalites have already harmed the feminine cause by demanding division of reservation for women along caste lines. This is the biggest danger because feminine problems are not class, caste or electorate specific, they are universal.

In the name of 'social justice', to keep fifty percent seats in the Parliament and other legislative bodies out of the women seats (whatever that percentage may be, thirty-three or less) marked out for women of OBC or ST/SC castes, is a devious ploy to keep women legislators under the thumb of parties already established as protectors of lower caste peoples. These saviours like Mulayam Singh Yadav, DMK, and Lalu Prasad are backward looking populists who shall install their own family women (like Lalu Prasad foisted his wife Rabri Devi as the Chief Minister of Bihar when he had to resign). What social change will this *bahu-beti* brigade bring to liberate women? Intellectually the 'social justice' crowd is a mix of outdated Marxists and Hindi/North India haters like the Southern party Dravida Munetra Kadgam (DMK) or they are parochial followers of R.M. Lohia and Jai Prakash Narain, again proponents of state controls and command economy. As said earlier, these castes are fascinated with aping the forward caste orthodoxies and are too conservative to negotiate fresh changes and cultural liberalism. Their alliance with the left parties reinforces conservatism and subjugation of women, known features of communist struggle all over the world. Neither in India nor elsewhere the Marxists have been able to produce women leaders. In this respect their record is as bad as that of Gandhi and the Hindu rightist. They are wiser than the BJP which made a public show of persecuting their own dynamic leader like Uma Bharti, but they have as few women in the Politbureau and other decision making bodies. So far the Congress has a better record of promoting women leadership and would have been a hope for India's women if it was not mired in dynastic clutches and intellectual paupery.

Women issues require decentralized movements of women organisations all over the country. Their leaders have to emerge from the grassroot movements that are not controlled by established political parties having no other interest than capturing power. There are several examples of women leadership emerging at the village level such as in the Chipko tree conservation movement in Uttaranchal and anti-liquor movements all over the country. But these women could not communicate with each other or make independent national forums of their own. Some of their leaders like Arundhati Roy and Medha Patkar are too dependent upon international support which brings them fame and awards but no expanding ground swell. Same is the story of a very large number of upper class anglophonic women activists who sooner or later are bonded to glamour chains in glitzy metropolitans as their funding comes not from India's small towns but international NGO's with dubious agendas.

If the greater participation of women in social and legislative sphere does not succeed in working for changes at the family and workplace level, the whole purpose of reservation of legislative seats for women stands defeated. A power hungry female of any species is no better than a power seeking male. Moralizing as it may sound, women have to demonstrate a greater creativity and constructive contribution ability than men. Merely replacing one sex by another does not ensure any advancement.

JANAPADA : Regional Defacement

13

Anglophonic Hegemony and Regional Indian Languages

The European Concept of the Nation State

The place of a language in a country depends upon how her people think about the modern nation state. The rise of the nation state, a rather recent political entity in history, was witnessed in Europe in the 18th century. The Euro-nation state was conceived on the basis of a linguistic territory that became more recognizeable after the spread of print culture. As long as language was a spoken phenomenon, the territory of a French or German language was hazy. But with printed books, newspapers and standardization style for a recognized public, the territory of the English, French or Italian became clearly visible and could be transformed into a political identity not available earlier. Combined with some other factors, such as the rise of middle class, recognition of democratic and proletarian dreams, notions of 'ethnic folk' or 'ethnic people', notions of a common cultural identity, a given language could be made the foundation of a nation state. Whereas in pre-modern days, the family line (royal or otherwise), religious sect, financial status and economic alliances made up the identity of a person, the nation state focused heavily on linguistic identity of her citizens.

This new fangled notion of the nation state was imposed upon a vast number of territories in Asia, Americas and Africa by the Euro-colonizers who upon their departure created new nations out of the occupied territories. For instance, with the redrawing of boundaries for Greece and Turkey, all Greek speakers had to leave Turkey and all Turkish speakers had to move out of Greece. Or as in India, Pakistan as an Urdu speaking Islamic State was carved out of the Hindu majority India that always has had many languages and diverse faiths. Former Soviet Union was split into many Central Asian countries, so was Yugoslavia into five nations. Although this caused immense misery to the populations, which were grouped and resettled on linguistic or religious basis, the European notions of ethnicity and nationhood have remained unchanged. Chechnya, Kashmir, Nagaland, Tamil Elam, and many other nations yet un-conceived, loom on the agenda of those who espouse this line of thinking. This bias of the Europeans is so deep-rooted and the urge to redraw territories so strong that many Asian countries feel a constant threat of dismemberment.

It is not surprising that according to the hardliners of this thought India is not one nation but a conglomeration of many nations all of which should be recognized as sovereign states. They feel that India is an imagined idea espoused by Indian or rather Hindu nationalists who are equating this imagined idea of a single national expanse called India with the territory that the British had occupied and called India. Hence they say, the British created India, which the Hindu nationalists are now trying to transform into a nation. Some of these Euro-centric thinkers grant that India has been created while others believe that it is never possible. Yet others say that India is a European Union like conglomeration but for the moment they do not advise dismemberment of the present day Indian State mainly because they do not wish the same to be prescribed for the EU.

Let us, however, examine if there have been other non-European but workable concepts of nationhood.

The Indian Nationhood

As distinct from glossocentric and historically recent Euro-nationalism, India had begun to think of herself as a nation very early. There is evidence that appellations such as the '*Jambudveepa*', '*bhaarata*', '*bharatakhanda*', or '*karma-bhoomi*' (portion of which was often called '*Aaryavarta*') were used to describe the geographic subcontinent of India, well before the Christian era. This was not imagined as a political entity or a religious expanse but nevertheless as a distinct cultural expanse that shared some fundamental notions of social organization, plurality, life-aims and good conduct and even lineage. This culturally territorial expanse of India extended in the West up to Persians (*paaras*) and Greeks (*yavanas*) and in the East up to the Chinese (*Cheenas*). They were distinctly defined as the outsiders because they did not follow the codes of Manu and others *dharma-sutrakaaras*. Many periphery cultures such as the *aabheera, dardara, gandharva, saindhava* etc., were acceptable as insiders.

In the first millennium, undoubtedly, the earlier cultural and philosophical notions of *varna, jaati, vamsha, pancha rina, shaastra-aachaara, loka-aachaara, purushaarthas*, were consolidated through a constant instruction of the standard texts: philosophical, literary, artistic and ethical texts called the *ithaahasa, puraanas, kaavyas*, and *shaastras* taught through a rigorous system of higher learning that was pan Indian. There was also the practice of utilitarian and fine arts that were patronized sub-continentally. Over and above the sacred sites of every religious sect, their holy river banks and mountains and forests extended all over the land and fostered an unabated movement and resettlement of pilgrims, students, performers and preachers.

The holy sites like Rameswaram, Dwaraka, Kashi, Gaya, or Pavapuri, thousands of miles away, have command since very early times and still command the same sense of belonging in an Indian as his or her place of settlement (*graama*), or origin (*moola*). The Indian obligation to travel to holy sites, or encourage and assist the travelers to these places, is much stronger than seen in other cultures. No wonder that with every passing occasion miraculous numbers gather at Kumbha and other pilgrimages. This sacred belonging of the Indian to the land as a whole cannot be underestimated even though it is beyond the grasp of modern secular notions of citizenship and state.

Political scientists working under Western paradigms cannot count upon sacredness of the land as a social unifier, just as the conquering Europeans could not understand why the American Indians could not sell their land because they considered it sacred.

This sacred bonding with whole of India cannot be dismissed as a phenomenon of the past as it is still a major driving force in the lives of Indian people who, including the poorest, overstrain their means and health to make these journeys. Most unfortunately, Nehruvian secularism failed to nurture pilgrimages and pilgrims and thus weakened national bonding and cultural flowering. Devaluation of religion as an article of political faith continues to debar India from using its inherited infrastructure of emotional growth, unity and richness.

Pre-colonial Use of Languages

In a land with a huge number of languages and dialects, political objectification of a single language for representing the identity of a state is impossible. Even small empires on the Indian soil had subjects speaking many languages and the mobility of populations; trade and travel have been much higher in India than in Europe or other continents. Besides, India has sparingly used the medium of writing, resulting in a lack of standardization of vernaculars and dialects. Thus, as a largely orality-based culture, polyglossia was an Indian necessity as well a fulfillment of its constant urge for diversity. One language for all purposes is a demand of the modern nation state. A different language for different purpose was the Indian way.

And so we find that while Sanskrit was used for mantra-conjoined rituals, intellectual discourse and higher education; the prakrits were used for music, dance, popular poetry, non-formal speech and simpler instruction. The best guide to who spoke which language for which purpose is found in the ancient plays. Unlike the ancient Greek or Roman theatre, Indian theatre was polyglossic. Instructions for multilingual usage in a single play are detailed by the *Natyashaastra*, which says that a play should reflect everyday social behavior. It establishes beyond doubt that even a moderately educated Indian was a polyglot and his attitude to language was utilitarian. Notions like 'mother-tongue' or 'official language' were non existent. The *Arthashaastra* nowhere mentions the choice of a particular language, let alone Sanskrit, as suited to needs of the state to be used as an official language. Edicts by the governments were issued not only in Sanskrit but in many languages.

Sanskrit indeed had a special place of regard as '*ati-bhaashaa*' because it had a vast repository of intellectual literature and was the language of the Vedas. But very early non-Vedic sects like Buddhism and Jainism patronized Pali and Magadhee respectively, which had the same sacredness for their adherents as Sanskrit for the Vedics. In fact all speech or *Vaak* was considered sacred if it had a valuable meaning. There was no concept of a national literature or a national language.

Other than plays, polyglossic essays or pieces called '*manipravaala*' were an esteemed literary genre. It was purely a practical approach to language that encouraged the bhakti poets to begin composing their songs in Tamil, Telugu and later in Hindi and all other medieval Indian languages. This tendency was inspired above all by Indian theater and performing arts, which had always used less Sanskrit and more Prakrit to truthfully communicate with the common people. Just as the *Naatyashaastra* was valued as the fifth Veda that brought the knowledge of the four Vedas to the ordinary folks, the prakrits and the vernacular poets also brought the knowledge of the Vedas and other deeper discourses in Sanskrit to the laity ('*beda mata sodhi sodhi, sodhi ke puraana mati*' as poet Beni described the enterprise of Tulsidas).

It may be pointed out that the antagonism between Sanskrit and Prakrit does not seem to leave much evidence in the first millennium. In fact, it was much later that certain medieval sects of *nirguna* and *nirmala bhakti* poets who ridiculed letters and learning and who seem to be anti-Sanskrit. These were no times for scholarship or an intellectual upsurge in any field. A general emphasis on otherworldliness had subdued every other activity and the *nirgunis* were not alone in ridiculing intellectualism. The acidic lines of some of these 'unlettered' ('*kaakad masi lakhyo nahi*') poets like Kabir should not be taken to be anti Sanskrit but as against dry intellectualism and hypocrisy.

Foreign Languages as Court Languages

In medieval India foreign languages became the royal or court languages for the first time. This reflected the distance between the people and foreign rulers. Sanskrit was no doubt an elite language but by no stretch of imagination disconnected with Indian languages. In fact it was nurturing them constantly by a continuous process of sanskritization. But the new class of monarchs and their aristocracy were the first conquerors that, unlike earlier conquerors, neither accepted the local faiths nor the culture. For the first several hundred years the frequent conflicts between indigenous cultures and a fanatic form of Islam was the order of the day. This aristocracy believed in their racial and religious superiority and considered the locals as well as the class of mixed blood as inferior. The angst of this mixed class born of foreign fathers and Indian mothers, is best expressed in Amir Khusro's (a mixed blood person) eulogy of Hindostani things that this class denigrated.

The advent of Turkish with the establishment of the Sultanate of Delhi threw up a new challenge that was met by the Indian mind through the creation of Urdu which drew upon from Arabic, Persian and other Central Asian tongues as well. It mediated between the rulers and the ruled and was not made the official language till very late. It was essentially the lower administrator's language and of the Sufi saints. All said and done it was an Indian product. It also worked well to negotiate with the new rulers who had settled here and created only a partial colonization. But there can be no mistake that foreign languages at the Court created the hiatus between the administration and people and this is unfortunately prevalent to this day in India. Indians accepted the hiatus created by English easily as they were used to this gap for the last many centuries.

The Colonial Imposition of English

The Islamic rulers did not wish to alter the indigenous Hindu judicial and educational systems, as there were limits to their power to enforce such a change. They established parallel systems for themselves and the Indian converts to Islam. Their strategy was only to obliterate and harm as much, the Hindu cultural institutions, when it was to be done for political conquest. But the British, with their heavy white man's burden had not only the Semitic notion of saving souls of the heathens but also the Enlightenment arrogance to replace the Indian educational, judicial and administrative systems with their own. With the new technology of the printing press and the policy of eliminating the traditional village *paathshaalaa* system, the traditional system of education along with the old curriculum was completely replaced by the European system. In the Islamic times, while Turkish, Persian or Arabic were required to be cultivated by only those close to the Islamic courts. The local *paathshaalaas* were available to those who wished to learn just enough for a vocation and *ashrams* for those going for higher learning, but in the British times learning a foreign language, namely English, was not a matter of choice but of compulsion as it was the only language of the new and the only educational system.

The change ushered in by the British rulers was both extensive and subtle. Islamic rule imposed a culture very little of which managed to percolate. Too often the barbarity of imposition created a strong resistance. In spite of their terribly exploitive rule, Muslims could not wipe out the Indian system of education. The British on the other hand, established Anglophonic hegemony not only by creating an official language but also a class of Indians, as planned by Macaulay, which had a deeper interest in maintaining this hegemony for its own survival and well being. Nehru, as we said, retained both the hegemony and the class.

Formation of Linguistic States in Independent India

Although from the middle of the 19th century with the new Europeanized system English began to attain enviable supremacy, nevertheless with the help of the printing press the Indian languages also underwent a process of standardization and modernization. They too reached a larger number of readers of the middle class. From the first to the fourth decade of the 20th century every Indian language can boast of great poets, novelists and writers and a huge number of books on a great variety of subjects. Regional literatures were indeed the main vehicles of creating and consolidating the Nationalist movement. In this enterprise the territory of the modern Indian languages and the identities of their speakers was also solidified. Along with Hindi, Bengali, Kannada and other literatures, came the recognition of Hindi, Bengali, Kannada and other 'people' and the identity of the regions or *pradeshas* where these people lived. In other words, the effect of print on the European soil was seen in India too, except that each '*pradesh*' was not thought of as a nation. The concept of Bharat, the land and Bharat Mata, the Mother of Indians which drew upon the earlier notions of a cultural unity of the subcontinent was strong enough to prevent that. The newly fabricated regional identities based on language were so strong that as early as 1938, the Nehru Report prepared by the Congress Party had declared that new regional states within the country would be formed on linguistic lines after Independence. And sure enough when the Commission for reorganization of states was appointed in the mid fifties it suggested their formation along linguistic lines. This did raise many fears and some opposition but on the whole the idea was a *fait accompli*. The whole debate of the times is summarized in a booklet *Thoughts on Linguistic States*, that the ailing BR Ambedkar, wrote at home as he could not debate the matter in the Indian Parliament. He thought that linguistic states are good for recognizing the identity of a regional people and their governance but he was apprehensive and suggested that the states should be small (otherwise the big ones shall dominate and UP shall always make a Prime Minister), and that there should be no mixed lingual state like the huge Madras and Bombay Presidencies carrying over from British India. Ambedkar was emphatic that all states should have Hindi as their official language and which should be so for the whole country:

> Linguistic State with its regional language as its official language may easily develop into an independent nationality. The road between an independent nationality and an independent State is very narrow. If this happens, India will cease to be Modern India we have and will become the medieval India consisting of a variety of States indulging in rivalry and warfare. This danger is of course inherent in the creation of linguistic States. There is equal danger in not having linguistic States. The former danger a wise and firm statesman can avert. But the dangers of a mixed State are greater and beyond the control of a statesman however eminent. How can this danger be met? *The only way I can think of meeting the danger is to provide in the Constitution that the regional language shall not be the official language of the State. The official language of the State shall be Hindi and until India becomes fit for this purpose English. Will Indians accept this? If they do not, linguistic States may easily become a peril.*

(1) The idea of having a mixed State must be completely abandoned.

(2) Every State must be a unilingual State. One State, one language.

(3) The formula one State, one language must not be confused with the formula of one language, one State.

(4) The formula one language, one State means that all people speaking one language should be brought under one Government irrespective of area, population and dissimilarity of conditions among the

> people speaking the language. This is the idea that underlies the agitation for a united Maharashtra with Bombay. This is an absurd formula and has no precedent for it. It must be abandoned. A people speaking one language may be cut up into many States as is done in other parts of the world.

What followed was not a thought out policy but the formation of states along linguistic lines according to the pressure that a region could mount through on the Center through violent agitation. It seems that during the first half of the 20th century and in the two decades of Independence, not only Nehru or Ambedkar but hardly any leader of consequence had an idea of total redundancy of forming linguistic states. At no period in Indian history, was language a basis for unity and at all times the polyglossic situation has prevailed strongly. However as in so many other things mimicking Europe was equated with modernity, and the linguistic states were carved out.

Throwing to the winds Ambedkar's warning that regional language should not be the official language, a three language formula for education and governance was evolved, namely regional language (also called mother-tongue) as first language at school and the regional state's official language, Hindi as link language (so called to reduce it from the status of the national language) to be used by the Center and English as the status quo language till the three language formula was implemented.

It is well known that the 'three-language formula' was not implemented in administration except half-heartedly. The actual consequential file work of the government continued in English and some notices at the center were issued in Hindi and regional languages in the state offices. In the schools and universities Hindi was taught compulsorily except in Tamil Nadu, which has observed a hate-Hindi ritual to fuel its Dravidianism.

With the advent of Independence and the formation of the linguistic states the earlier desire to serve the languages and use them for the literary and administrative use of the nation was replaced by the quest for power and the Indian languages were used as instruments for that aim. While the regional languages got bitterly involved in negotiating their status against Hindi (which is more of a declared than a practicing official language in the country), in day to day practice English even handedly marginalized all languages of India including Hindi and Sanskrit, not only for maintaining itself as the bureaucratic tongue but as the medium of judiciary, scientific research, medicine and every other kind of intellectual writing, speech and higher education. The net result of the contest between Hindi and other languages was a serious decline in the growth and status of each and every language of India. While in the pre-Independence era, literary writing in all Indian languages and even their dialects touched great heights, after Independence in spite of the greater awareness of the bigger world, quality of regional writing went down in talent. In less than three decades, English writing far excelled the regional works and became notable on a global scale.

From Anglo-Raj to Anglophonic Socialism

The main reason for building the hegemony of English has been an elitism that is nurtured by the Indian notions of tradition (*paramparaa*) that urges the new rulers to emulate their predecessors. The anglophones got away by enforcing an aura of the importance of English on the gullible Indian middle class. Under the Socialist state when notions of excellence was dictated by state controlled universities and elite institutions, this was an easy task. The anglophones have been adept at giving all sorts of reasons to show the superiority of English as a universal language that can keep India pulsating along with international change. The stock phrase was coined by Nehru who called English as 'the window to the outer world' and devised an under the surface status quo to keep his government as the inheritor of British Raj. He kept the Raj going by simply prefixing the deceptive word 'national' to the name of every institution created by the British while all institutions kept the colonial aloofness and the bureaucratic superiority that the British had devised to govern India.

The English language was a major medium of keeping this distance between the rulers and ruled and Nehru deliberately maintained it. His Socialist State was as much in need of a domineering bureaucracy. Other than for labour and small business, the State was also the biggest employer in the country. As it demanded a working knowledge of English, anglophonic hegemony was easily ensured. Ironically, the doctrine of socialism that espouses power to the masses surpassed every country of the world in creating a vast army of foreign language speaking state employees. The hegemony of English is a direct consequence of the Socialist regime. If India has chosen a competitive capitalist road, the diversity of business and employment would have used the Indian languages in all their diversity.

Globalization Promotes Polyglossia

After the digital revolution and the globalization of capital and labor through the Internet, anglophones imagine English to be the glossiest feather in their cap. No doubt, the innumerable English medium schools made it possible for its students to migrate to greener pastures and the less luckier ones to work in BPO (business process outsourcing centers) attending to global customers. But this is a rather small part of the burgeoning young population that still faces acute unemployment. For the majority of the people who do not need a window to the outer world such as English but who work in their languages only, hegemony of English is an obstruction or a beating stick wielded by bureaucracy and the elite.

So far in one decade of globalization we have seen only the rewards of having a big English knowing population. But the huge market that regional Indian languages' speakers provide to the consumer products from all over the world is yet to be tapped. Very special multilingual skill would be required from the masters of business management in years to come. We have already seen that Hollywood English films are translated and subtitled into Hindi and Tamil and so forth. Such translation skills are needed for books, cartoon, videos and a number of products as the middle class grows in India. The Nehruvian policies were determined by the command economy and state stranglehold over schools and universities.

However, with the greater privatization of higher education, diversity of curriculum at all levels, the utilitarian approach to education and hence language is destined to replace these strangleholds. The corporate world is still dominated by products of anglophonic and ivy-league alumni that have not yet realized the indigenous shift on the horizon.

A new commercial growth in India free from state controls promises rosier days for the Indian languages. It is not going to be a situation where offices and schools were the only venues for clerks and teachers of Hindi, Punjabi and the state recognition of a language was indexed by the number of street signs in it. Not the compulsory Hindi at schools but the Hindi cinema and Hindi television has promoted the language across the land. The television revolution cashed upon the little known fact that while forty percent of Indians are Hindi speakers, eighty percent are passive listeners and can hence receive and comprehend Hindi.

The emergence of Hinglish (a mixture of Hindi and English, a sort of Anglordu) on the television suggests that the Shakespeare spouting government officer is a creature of the past.

A polyglot with as many languages as possible is likely to be a better and more popular functionary both in the government and in business.

With the formation of many states like Uttaranchal, Jharkhand, and Chattisgarh, and Telangana, Bundelkhand and Vidarbha in the pipeline, Ambedkar's formula of many states with one language has become a reality. Many states have also recognized some languages as their second and third languages. Delhi state has given an official status to Punjabi and Urdu. Thus with the state more or less working in English and giving token recognition to more than one language and with the wider use of Hindi (opposition to it being restricted to pious riots in Tamil Nadu where they immolate themselves while Kerala folks learn Hindi and get employed all over the land), the actual utilitarian approach to languages shared in India since time immemorial is emerging. The rise of digital technology is an also auspicious event for polyglossia. Transcription and even translation is going to become cheap and widespread. Greater flexibility and freer choice to the students should be the new policy in schools. What we need is enthusiastic patronization of the languages from the Indian people and minimum interference by the governments.

14

The Frigid Face of Urdu

Time and again impassioned pleas to save Urdu come from all quarters. Parliamentarians like Mr. Banatwala thunder about the step-brotherly treatment thrust upon Urdu; Mr. Shahabuddin laments the decline of Urdu press and the shrinking strength of its students. The Congress has always extolled this fountain of *ganga-jamuni* culture, but done little beyond. When in power the BJP considered it judicious to let an eminent Kathak dancer refocus on Ghalib in the lanes old Delhi. Whatever the quarter, the attitude is conservationist. Its proponents equate its development with jobs for its graduates. But there is hardly any effort to make it more useful in the contemporary scene. What has been forgotten is the force which gave it birth, growth and resilience, namely its erstwhile vitality to interact and mix with other languages; its historical usefulness for the lower middle class to communicate with corridors of power and high tradition when rulers prided in Turkish, Persian and Arabic.

Urdu was never the language of the elite or the masses. It is difficult to convey this bit of linguistic history to modern Indians or even Pakistanis as false stories about languages and scripts are a powerful influence. Many well educated people have to be told that Sanskrit was not always written in Devanagari before the nineteenth century, but in all the scripts associated with regional languages today. One script for one language is a creation of print technology. Films like Mughle-Azam and a host of TV serials that thrust Persianised Urdu into the mouth of every Muslim character from king to fisherman or chaste Hindi (Sanskrit infested) into the speech of every Hindu, have left no room for linguistic history in the common imagination.

Urdu was also not the official or court language in medieval India except at the sunset of the Mughal empire. The place was occupied mostly by Persian. As is well known Urdu began as a pidgin in the eleventh century with the interaction between the local Hindi that prevailed at the time. The sufis used it to create their syncretic expression for devotees of mostly the lower classes. Its early literature was a mixture of medieval Hindi, from Dingal to Brij, Avadhi, Punjabi and Mewari etc. The *sufiana kalaam* extant today got refurbished in the process of aural transmission and musical performances. Across the Vindhyanchal it developed as *dakkhini*.

> Using different languages in a single text or composition is an age old tradition in India. Ancient plays used Sanskrit, Shaurseni, Magadhi etc., all together. Compositions with some lines in Sanskrit and some in Prakrit constituted the *manipravala* style. Sufis carried forward this tradition by mixing lines of Brij and Persian. Centuries later in the twilight of Aurangzeb's rule, *Dakkhini* and *Khari Boli* were heavily weighed down by Persian-Arabic vocabulary and imagery to make a style which is regarded as elite or *adabi* glossary of Urdu. Wali, Mir, Bedil and Dard consolidated this style in Delhi; Insha, Sauda and others in Lucknow.

> Further into the nineteenth century when parochialism and ornamentation became rampant in all arts and cross country movement of artists obtaining earlier under Mughal patronage came to an end, Urdu poetry leaned too heavily on Persian. Yet it was not distinguished generically from Hindi. Dreaming of attaining immortality through his Persian poetry, Ghalib called his vernacular writing *kalame-hindavi* loaded with all the topographic ambivalence of the word *hind.*

The advent of print marked out Urdu as visually separate. By the end of the last century, the elitist Urdu of the court poets of the last emperor and the *Luknawi* literati, was slowly given an ethnic connotation by the western sociological system in which groups are defined by the building blocks of religion, language, script, food and clothes. In another half a century, the nexus of Islam-Urdu-Arabic script-nonvegetarianism-*salwar-kameez* was formalised. Urdu was no longer a medium of approaching the new ruling class and its language (now English), or other languages of India as in the past. The westernised Urdu elite, not the lower middle class, now called the shots. Urdu became the medium of constructing modern Muslim identity and also a separate nation. This is evident most in the fact that the Urdu of All India Radio is no different (except for the accent) from that of Radio Pakistan. In both the countries formal Urdu shrinks from contact with Sindhi, Punjabi, Hindi, Gujarati and Marathi. Movement by some writers on both side of the border to make it open and flexible receives little encouragement.

Identity phobia in persons, traditions, and languages generates first frigidity and then hostility towards others.

Collections of great Urdu poets are sold in Devanagari editions in huge numbers. Some day an Urdu newspaper may try to experiment by giving two pages in Devanagari, or a Hindi daily may experiment with two Urdu pages. The script is a matter of technology and should be left to evolve as per demand in all Indian languages. Exchanges between languages make them richer and stronger. It is more a matter of attitude, whether to be open or close minded. The point (*nuktaa*) of identity if pushed too far can isolate (*judaa*) us from even God (*khudaa*) let alone other beings but if used judiciously, it can end our egoism (*josh*) and bring sanity (*hosh*).

15

What is Ethnic?

There seems to be a wide spread fear among the white majority nations that the twenty-first century will witness extensive cultural conflicts. Professor Samuel Huntington of Harvard University has been one of the eminent proponents of this view and his forecasts regarding the conflict with Islam has come true. While one need not underestimate the dangers of cultural conflicts, the very definition of ethnic and its manipulation by Western anthropological thought also needs to be examined thoroughly.

'Ethnos' in Greek was used for indicating a community which need not have been a tribe or a community of civilisationaly simpler kind. The ancient city of Athens in the golden age consisted of twelve major 'ethnoi.' They were not only equal citizens of the 'polis', they were also civilizationally equal insiders to its cultural milieu. However, their differences of descent, lineage, cults and wealth did not prompt them to make separate political groups within the urban and rural areas of Athens. An 'ethnos' was a consanguine group which could exert political pressure for its interests but which never thought of itself as a political entity. The best parallel to the Greek 'ethnos', is the Sanskrit idea of *jati*, which denotes a subcommunity within a larger culture, having distinct qualities on account of economic, professional or ritual differences.

Ethnicity: A Colonial Definition

The ancient Greek word 'ethnos', acquired a very different connotation when it was used by modern European anthropologists and sociologists for describing civilisations under colonial domination. 'Ethnos', came to denote a non European, civilisationally less complicated community (as in South America, Africa or Australia), or a less technocratised society (as in Asia or China), which was also objectified as the Other of the white man.

As the colonial powers had approached other cultures primarily to ensure their political subjugation, they developed a methodology of giving cultural definitions that relied, not on cultural parametres, but on political and administrative premises. Culture was seen as means of marking out and limiting group entities. For the facility of administrators, behaviour patterns of the administered cultures were stereotyped by historians and sociologists and the colonised people were expected to behave according to these patterns. To help the maintainance of social and political status quo, it was postulated that by and large the non-European cultures were centripetal by nature and they made their people inward looking, groupish, traditional, and ritualistic.

Therefore, the prime purpose of an 'ethnos', or a *jati*, was defined as preservational and promotive of culture by self-enclosure. It is no wonder that historians like A. L. Basham repeatedly asserted that caste in India was very helpful in preserving its cultural heritage, particularly in times of external invasions.

During the colonial period ethnography helped to contain and manipulate the populations, but after its end, ethnography was used to perform new functions. Most colonisers succeeded in propogating that the territory held by them could not be administered by the indigenous people as they were not one nation but a conglomerate of many nations. It was postulated that the basis of nationality for the non-Europeans was the 'ethnos', and that every ethnic group is either actually a nation or has the potential of becoming one, and therefore, should have its own sovereign government. So, while it was all right for the British to be a nation (with all its Scottish, Welsh and other minorities) and to rule India, on their withdrawal, India had to be divided into two distinct 'ethnic' groups, India, the Hindu majority nation and Pakistan, the Muslim nation.

Euro-view of Culture

There have been two reasons behind the construction of this definition of ethnicity by Eurocentric anthropology. One is the belief, that culture is not primarily a way of organising and preserving knowledge and skills of life, but is a strategy for creating power structures. The second, derived out of the first, is the view that nationalism rests upon cultural distinctions (such as language or religion) to mark out a population for a nation state. This was also the logic behind the creation of nation states in Europe through the last four centuries. Culture was their best instrument for political organisations and power hierarchies and that is this belief which Europe (and its intellectual offspring, America) have been busy foisting upon the rest of the world. Long after the end of major colonial governments, ethnography is still in big business. Once an 'ethnos' is well demarcated by the Eurocentric scholarship from the populations of the Asian or African regions, it does not take very long to convince its people that their 'ethnos' is not just a tribe or a sub-group but a nation which should be and can be a sovereign state. If the cultural distinctions of language, religion or customs were the basis of nationalism in Europe, it should also be so for the rest of the world. (Even the modern Greeks have accepted 'ethnos' as a synonym for nation and 'ethnikismos' for nationalism).

Nowadays a centripetal image of the ethnic way of life is highlighted and sometimes projected as superior and more rewarding than the centrifugal, rationalist, and open minded European societies. The mutual dependence of the ethnic groups or communities, within their broad cultural expanse is under-played and the common conceptual ground beneath their diversified beliefs is also pushed out of view. As a result, many cultural groups, which under the precolonial order, never thought of claiming any distinct ethnic individuality on grounds of minor differences, are now being made to believe in their uniqueness and thus claim separate political identities out of the erstwhile homogenous and interactive regional populations.

The Sikhs, for instance, were always considered a sect within the general umbrella of Hinduism until the beginning of this century. But after the penning of Sikh history and philosophical tenets by the English historians and religiographers, it is now taken for granted, even in India, that the Sikhs are not Hindus. This recasting of the Sikh identity has contributed to the turmoil in the Punjab leading to the demand of a sovereign homeland for the Sikhs.

Similarly, the hypothetical existence of an Aryan race, that supposedly swept down from the Nordic North or Caspian Asia, first into Greece, then into Iran, and finally into India to oust from the Gangetic plains the Dravidian inhabitants of the Indian subcontinent, has had a disastrous impact on modern Indian politics. Even though there is hardly any evidence of a distinct Dravidian race in terms of physical anthropology, nonetheless on the basis of linguistic differences, the South Indian Tamils have used the Aryan-Dravidian-Divide theory to practice an aggressive Tamil nationalism that has spawned terrorist strife in Ceylon and hysterical provincialism in Tamil Nadu.

'Ethnic' is Europe's Other

One can go on citing innumerable examples of the divisive impact of Euro-American ethnology on the socio-political life of colonised cultures which under Eurobrainframing has totally reconstructed their histories (now called factual accounts) in opposition to their indigenous mythic constructs. Whereas the economically weaker regions of the world are breaking into ethnically reorganised states, the technologically superior and financially stronger nations of Europe and North America have quite successfully resisted the fissiparous demands from within (such as those of the French Canadians or the native Americans, the Spanish Basques) and have progressed towards a consolidated Europe. The break up of the Soviet Union into a number of Central Asian nations has been hailed as freedom for the erstwhile ethnic groups living under the Soviet yoke. But a proposal to make half a dozen independent nations for the American Indian natives out of the territory of the USA and Canada for the sake of the utterly oppressed peoples living in the suffocating confines of American Indian Reservations will be interpreted as a plot to dismember North America.

It is obvious then, the whole construct of the ethnic is only for categorizing non-Eurogenic cultures, and that an ethnic population is entitled to sovereignty only if it exists outside the Euro-American territories. Within Euro-America it has no such rights. There, it is supposed to find a niche for itself under the grand cultural mosaic, where the white hand arranges the diverse coloured pieces into the pattern it deems best. In other words, nationalism, like older technology, is now for the consumption of poorer nations. For the leaders in technology and economic power, there is the post-national intermixture of global commerce. At this point it may be relevant to point out that in the eyes of the so called ethnic peoples, the culture of Euro-Americans is just another ethnic group, which can more appropriately be called leuko-ethnic. If all those premises which are used to categorise an 'ethnos' in Asia are used upon Euro-Americans, there is no reason why they cannot be categorised as people with well demarcated behaviour patterns that which constitute the Other of the ethnic population of the world. In other words, it is also important to realise that if we persist in the present methodology of ethnic categorisation, the world will end up getting divided into two major categories, the ethnic and the leuko-ethnic. Already the signs of this divide are looming large. Perhaps the likes of Professor Huntington have already sensed this divide but are not admittting it. Their predictions of ethnic strife, are perhaps, a euphemism for an impending confrontation between the Euro-Americans and the remaining societies of the world, between the possessors of advanced technologies and the techno-havenots.

II

The ethnological categorisation of the non-European cultures would have ended very well for the Leuko-ethnics, if the migration of the work force from the so called ethnic world into the West had not taken place at a very large scale. Moreover, the ever growing impact of information technologies has created new equations that are taking an unpredictable course. The "natives" are no longer out there in the lands where the white man could have borne their burden at a safe distance. They are now permanently lodged in London, New York, Paris, Chicago and in so many other bastions of Western commerce. What is worse, they have brought with them not only the cultural Other, but also a host of political conflicts that rage in their lands of origin. The redistribution of populations is taking place not only on account of the adventurous seeking greener pastures but much more so on account of populations getting displaced by war and internal strife. There are an estimated four and a half million refugees, mostly from Asian countries, now residing in Europe, says a report from the Office of the United Nations High Commissioner for Refugees. There is little doubt that in coming years, though the developed nations may close their doors on immigrants, they would not be able to contain the number of refugees which is going to increase as internal conflicts within the nations on their borders or even across sea straights are on the rise. Not only the wealthier nations but the poorer ones are also going to receive refugee populations. A slow trickle of migrants from Bangladesh into India has been an irreversible trend in the last two decades. If the Sind province of Pakistan flares up very badly in the near future, refugees can even pour into India .

Ethnic goes Global

As the older notion of national loyalty is breaking, in the coming years people would not hesitate to apply for refugee status when the going gets tough or insecure in their motherlands. They will depend more and more on members of their community settled in better off nations to support them directly or covertly. Formation of NGOs at a large scale, with infotechs at their command has begun to play a major role in private and non-governmental group communication. This has rapidly brought about a politicisation of the ethnic communities who are paying less attention to updating the practices of their living cultures but more to institutionalised agitation to seek advantages within a Eurocentric cultural milieu of standardised and individualised consumerism. Power of the information technologies has provided new political strategies. The latest strategy is the tendency of the politicians to globalise local issues. Nowadays, a local issue only needs to be splashed repeatedly on the media to make it global. And if the issue concerns a regional strife, violent acts are the best means of drawing attention. As modern tastes go, acts of violence make the most media friendly news. Little wonder that terrorism is becoming increasingly popular and so called ethnic strifes like in Iraq, or Iran, Sri Lanka or Pakistan are getting less controllable. Terrorism now flourishes, not only because of the big ammunition trade, but because it is also the cheapest way to seize attention.

There is no escape now from evolving a new cultural anthropology for global harmony, the premises of which would have to come from non-Euro-American cultures. We now need to turn away from the modern habits of individualism, sensationality and mass indulgence. In this endeavour of forging new values, nothing can be more helpful than the pre-Aristotelian Greek and the Upanishadic Indian thought. These philosophies can help us to prepare a new ground through ethical courage (arete), devotion (eulabeia), self-analysis (*atmanavesana*), and unpossesiveness (*aparigraha*). More than any others, these are the values now needed to evolve new cultural constructs and balanced social structures. But more than just choosing certain values we need to revise our whole analysis of human nature and values. Contemporary disbelief in the possibility of any universal substratum for human behaviour has pushed us into a morass of private and individual choices. The consequences of this Relativism are obvious in the form of loneliness and emotional fragmentation that has very nearly ended all deeper communication between the peoples. As a schizophrenic move, escape is being sought in globalism which is promoted as uniform behaviour. But present day globalism based on leukoethnic hegemony cannot bridge the gap between so called ethnic societies, or avoid " a clash of civilisations". We need a world culture which is affirmative of global diversity. For this we also need a fresh theory for studying cultures, arts, philosophies and ways of life, that are prevalent now and those that have achieved great heights of refinement in the past. In short, what is required is a fresh theory of cultural comparison and exchange.

III

The comparative-culture enterprise is still not a mainstream activity and is beset with many difficulties inspite of the present day hype on pluralism and information explosion. The big talk about global culture is totally deceptive. It is becoming exceedingly obvious, that there is no real attempt at creating a new global way of life that aims to draw from all the cultures of the world. On the contrary, there is the unstated expectation that the American way of development is a model that should be emulated all over the world, and with the help of the latest weapon called "information highway", the Euro-American culture should engulf the entire globe.

Debased Globalism

The process of uniformising and packaging is reducing the diversity of cultural symbols into mechanical signs that function as lowest common denominators. Local cultures are reduced to a grist to be consumed by the mill of global business. Cultures are now considered useful only if they provide minor and safe variations to the monotony of mass production. They are patronised only so far they can lend themselves to appropriation by global business. The strategies of appropriation are given attractive names and justifications and propagated as paradigms of emerging cultural harmony.

For instance, in the United States, the paradigm of the Melting Pot was once pushed very actively. The Melting Pot theory presumed that cultural diversity can easiliy be melted away to forge a harmonious life of the future of America. But this strategy was resisted by the non-white Anglo-Saxon components of the American society as it threatened their identity. When it created too many tensions, then a softer strategy was proposed, namely, that of the Cultural Mosaic. Ostensibly the Cultural Mosaic theory was designed to protect and promote the identities of non-white societies. The anthropological thrust of this period of theorising was to revive in-depth studies of the Asian and African societies which were projected as unchanging, closed, "structured", i.e., fixed identities contrasting with the dynamic, evolving and evoluting Euro-American societies. The very term "structure" (whether refering to the "deep" mental substratum or the "outer" physical organisation of societies and their behavior), was meant to denote fixity, and the theory of the Cultural Mosaic was supposed to allow a respiteful space to the many Others, the many coloured unchanging pieces, to survive within the American continent so that the Mosaic makers could play with the coloured pieces and patternize them at their will. Whereas the Melting Pot, dealt with differences by promoting uniformity, the Mosaic theory aimed to contain them by the inverse strategy of promoting self-centeredness and structured identity of the ethnics. Nevertheless, the glorification of the ethnic, also came to a dead end, as it was found to be a backward looking, museumising and an expensively ornamental enterprise.

Fortunately for the West, the info-technologies have provided a new opening which has revived the Melting Pot theory in a new packing. It has replaced the American Continent with the globe itself, and American nationalism with hyper-Internationalism, of course, covertly taking for granted that Internationalism cannot be but just another kind of Americanism.

Presentism

Adding to the phenomena of globalisation and commercialised ethnicity, there is something much more discouraging to a comparatist. And that is an unabashed emphasis on what may be called a post-modernist 'presentism' which creates a frame of mind which in some ways harkens to the Romantics. Despite a devaluation of Humanistic anthropocentricity by recent Continental philosophies, the post-industrial societies are not willing to accept the bleak limitations of the human condition which were once taken for granted by classical cultures. The brash optimism of the nineteenth century based on fetishes like 'progress', 'utopia', or 'new frontiers', is still haunting the Euro-American cultures in the shape of globalisation and market economy. This optimism endows the present-day human achievements with a teleology that is quite at variance with the preferences of ancient cultures which are nowadays regarded as fatalistic or other-worldly.

For the modern man, studies of the past societies have often been exercises in reconstructing the past according to the prejudices of the present. History, thus, often becomes a story rewritten, a mythos retold, to serve new values. For example, in the nineteenth century, European historians thought of ancient Greek culture as the progenitor of a rationalist, scientific and democratic values that gave birth to the city states. In reality, this writing of Greek history was more to buttress the European faith in modern nation states, colonialism and the philosophy of natural sciences.[1] Similarily, in order to provide a predecessor for European theatre, Greek theatre was imagined to be a logocentric performance by post-Renaissance Europe.[2] To take another example, modern Indian historians in their nationalist fervour portrayed ancient India as somewhat of an egalitarian and democratic society and underplayed its acute hierarchies, while the Marxist section of Indian historians wrote on the same period exaggerating its class struggles and economic disparities. The task of the comparatist, therefore, is to make the best effort to overcome the prejudicial impact of the present and view the past in its own terms of reference. This is a tall order considering that major trend of thought nowadays propagates that all signs, including language, have no core of meaning that can survive time or the user's subjectivity.

Agonism

There is not only the bias of time as a pitfall for the comparatist but also the bias of space that separates the objects of comparison. In space, the local is always evaluated as superior to the cultures beyond the territiory of the local. The Greeks looked down upon the 'barbaroi', the Indians upon the 'mlecchas' of the various kinds, while the Europeans have a history of devaluing 'natives', 'savages', 'primitives', and now the 'ethnics'. Sometimes these 'other people' are regarded as inferior in order to provide a justification for one's military, colonial or mono-polistic designs. At other times they are denigrated in cultural terms. The emphasis, in any case, is always on the differences and thus on the inferiority of the other. No wonder 'xenophobia' is a much used word, but 'xenophilia' is hardly ever used. The bias of space is agonal. New technologies not with standing, it has turned the present day cultural pluralism into a global strife as pluralism today is made to rest on promoting and asserting differences. As a result pluralism has helped more than anything else, sale of armaments and trade monopolies.

Samvada or Cultural Consonance

How can the comparatist overcome the two biases of time and space, of 'presentism' and 'agonism' (if these can be the names for theories that assist cultural strife and historical prejudices), to make meaningful bridges. The task can begin only by locating a common ground between targets of comparison because commonality and not differences are the *raison d'etre* of communication. If communication is to be something more than exchange of goods or info-commodity, then we may benefit most from turning to an old definition of communication called 'samvada'. "*Ekatrasya tu anyatra darsanam samvadah*" (When a thing existing at one place, is seen at another place, this phenomenon is called *samvada*). This is done by locating a core of vibrant similarity between the two objects of comparison, a similarity that exists beneath all differences and which, instead of being wiped out by the individual differences, sustains itself and the differences as well. To provide a simile, it is like the consonance between two musical notes, which are always independent but are always capable of generating a mutual resonance by virtue of their common grounding in a given scale. Within our pluralism we need to explore our common scale.

The *samvada* theory rests upon the postulation that differences rest or stand on common ground. Differences cannot exist all by themselves. In other words, the One creates the many, the Scale creates the notes. Identities are meaningful only so long as they interact, as do the musical notes in relation to one another. Cultures are vibrant only when they reveal their consonances. Otherwise, they stagnate or become violent, leading both ways to self-destruction. We need to have a fresh look at creating consonances, call for harmony, and oppose hegemony which has been our cultural purpose for so long.

Notes

1. In his *Early Greek Philosophy*, first published in 1892 and reprinted till 1930, J.Burnet says, ". . . a new thing came into the world with early Ionian teachers — the thing we call science... science has never existed except among people who have come under the influence of Greeks", p 31.
2. For a detailed discussion on this refer to, *Dramatic Concepts: Greek and Indian*, Delhi, D.K.Printworld, 1994, pp 6-12.

16

Cultural Nationalism
Kitsch or Charisma

In his deep desire to make Hindus learn something worthwhile from Islam, a general secretary of the Bhartiya Janata Party once declared that his party shall include into the new proposed common civil code the Islamic practice of formally seeking the consent of the woman at time of her marriage. The Hindu marriage ritual, he said, does not have such a provision and as an example of taking good things from all religions this seemed to be a good choice. As election eve is the only time for our legislators to think on religious rituals, what else is to be expected. In the marriage season they are too busy hoping from one *kalyanam* to another, blessing the newly weds and more so protecting their guardians from the tax-man who may question the expenses on the huge *pandals.* Do they ever stay to see the ceremony? If the BJP spokeman had stayed to attend, he would have learnt that much more than the consent, there are seven promises (*saptapadim kritvaa vaamam dakshinam tathaa*) that the bride extracts from the groom before she takes her rightful place at his side and before they are declared man and wife. This is not to suggest that Hinduism has nothing to learn from Islam or vice-versa, but certainly to point out that customs, rituals and family laws, of any sect for that matter, cannot be modernised or even civily codified by amateurish reforms.

Unending Tokenism

The weighty task of evolving a unified/common civil code to reflect a common cultural heritage, along with the revival of nationalism through cultural assertion against the renewed intrusion of Westernization through information technology has been taken upon its shoulders by the BJP. In priniciple this is a highly admirable venture and only the die-hard secularist rhetorician who advocates total unconcern of the state in religious life of the people can oppose it. But in practice the BJP has still to demonstrate its ability and even sincerity to execute it. So far the record of the party including its predecessor Jan Sangh and the synergic organisations of the Parivar has been poor. Even if one is ready to give the benefit of doubt and accept their sincerity, their ability and strategy show that without a major reorientation they shall not be able to revitalise the cultural life of the nation. Like the Congress and the Leftists who have done their best to fossilise the minorities by generating in them a constant identity-loss phobia, the BJP has worked on the Hindu majority religious sentiment through a tokenism that generates a false euphoria of cultural elation.

In the fifties the party agitated for an all India ban on cow-slaughter, but in the decades to follow it undertook to lead no movement among the masses for the improving the lot the cow by creating greater respect and care for the animal. The party could have floated a "*go-seva-dal*", helped set up research organisations for better breeding, asked for tax-holidays for cow-dairies and so forth. In short it could have combined the traditional Hindu devotion to the cow with modern technology for a healthier *govamsha*. But that needed something more than tokenism.

In the sixties and seventies the BJP was strong on pushing Hindi politically, but it did not create any institute of national excellence to promote Hindi as literature and as a medium for press, film, television and translation between other Indian languages. The funding for such enterprises need not always come through *sarkari* academies of the Centre or the States, it can come from the people as well as it did for Banaras Hindu University and Aligarh Muslim University when they were established. But the BJP wanted the change to come not through transformation at grass-root level but through state edicts that enforce the ideology of the party. Again, more than mere tokenist sloganeering, it required going to the people at ground level in large numbers in a sustained manner.

In the eighties the BJP did so for the cause of the Ram Mandir at Ayodhya at the Babri Masjid site. The workers of the RSS and all the Parivar were overactive at all the local temples across the nation to raise funds and as well as political support. It was the next major movement in India perhaps after *Bhudan Yajna* of Vinoba Bhave. But it had two inherent pitfalls. One, that it was reaction to Mandalisation and two that it can be a blind alley even if it succeeds. Even if you succeed in making the temple, no matter what the cost, then what ? One temple, however, marvellous cannot sustain Hindu culture all over the land. It is a figment of a biased imagination that can claim that by the controversy and confrontation it has so far generated "India's banished Hindu identity has staged a powerful comeback." It could have been so, had the BJP launched a nation wide program to improve thousands of Hindu temples, big and small, in villages and metros, to be cleaned, repaired, readministered, managed by the educated devotees and well trained priests and made into centres of art. It is the sanctuary around the corner that gives me my daily solace, not the great Kashi, Jersusalem or Mecca that are visited once in a lifetime. We need not one but a thousand sacred sites, and that is why our land is strewn with so many pilgrimages, and it is not enough to make one site a matter of Hindu identity (*Hindu asmita kaa savaal*). If Ayodhya struggle could be really so, that is a grass-root reform to be undertaken at thousands of shrines and not mere tokenism, the BJP would not have put it on the back burner so soon.

Very often we witness a blitzkreig by self appointed custodians of morality to prohibit display of affection in public places. Are such diktats in the interest of restrained moral conduct or are they well considered measures against Westernisation? Often a women's College principal orders that girl students shall not wear jeans and tops, (not specified if baggy ones will do). Such a principal often argues that she is imposing a code for decent dressing as jeans send wrong signals to conservative men and arouse their eveteasing instincts. Whether she does not want her students to fringe the fashion change and thus spare her the problems of campus conflicts, or her definitions of modesty require well covered (virtual purdah) bodies in conventional clothing or she insists on the *desi*-ness of dress to keep away global influences, is not easy to make out inspite of her many clarifications.

To Ape or Not to Ape

The non-Western societies are today faced with the dilemma of either aping the Euro-american model of amoral demagogy or reviving their religious roots with its acompanying pitfalls of obscurantism, commercial messiahism and the cultural packaging by half-baked gurus. There is also the third road, of promoting open and sustained dialogue between various cultural and religious groups and letting the fresh practices evolve among the people through a lived consensus instead of the state appointed votaries of culture giving the definitions and laws for national behaviour. Culture is not a matter of prescription that academics, bureaucrats and least of all, legislators can provide. One can create conditions for its flowering by education and patronage to discussion and debate, by encouraging its growth through sanctity and respect for a variety of discourse to be conducted less at the behest of the state but more by the zest of the scholars by encouraging the people to leave the rut and make new ways. If this ferment of reviving culture touches the people of the land, it must inevitably touch its Hindu majority, most of all to galvanise the nation. Is that not a more efficacious and genuine way for the "banished Hindu identity to stage a powerful comeback" with much more of creation (*mandana*) than the unending refutation (*khandana*) of others.

17

Religious Plurality in Education

"Pluralism" is a word that these days abounds alike in the glib talk of undergraduates, outpourings of subaltern film-makers, papers read by academics in international seminars and the maiden speeches of newly elected legislators. But do we usually pause to think:

1. What exactly do we mean by the word 'pluralism'?
2. What obligations and social conduct does a life of pluralism demand from its professed adherents?
3. Is pluralism a contemporary concept or have the older cultures also thought of it?
4. Does the present day world has capacity to manage variety and differences and still maintain a faith in the deeper unity of humankind?

It is a pity that on this earth where plurality has been debated in metaphysical and ethical terms for thousands of years, plurality has been now debased to mean merely a tolerance of diverse faiths and cultural habits. Discussions on plurality in the context of the ultimate nature of the seen and unseen universe are no longer the order of the day. Can the diversity of dress codes, sexuality, religious convictions, and morals be practiced if the finer questions of philosophical plurality are shoved under the carpet? Reducing the larger expanse of plurality and limiting it to the sphere of "ethnic tolerance" or "community harmony" is putting the cart before the horse. If the deeper springs of religious and social beliefs are not studied, debated, and analyzed, measures to keep the adherents of these faiths and communities in harmony are not going to succeed. Religious and cultural denominations will always be taken over by chest-beating demagogues who shall proclaim the right to dictate their whims on behalf of vast populations. Their conflicting claims shall continue to create recurring flare-ups in the name of identity protection and continue to detract from the deeper sources of spiritual and intellectual probing.

Pluralism is more than External Marks

The real worth of pluralism lies in making new and distinct choices off the beaten road. These differences created by the new choices should be profound investigations and not matters of mere practical conveniences or egotistical assertions. For example, in medieval India, the teachings of Nanak Dev, the first Guru of the Sikh denomination of Indic religions, provided a fresh method of infusing mantra repetition (*japa*) and community service in the non-iconic (*nirguna*) tradition of the devotional (*bhakti*) movement that invited adherents to his path from various religious denominations including the Muslims. Nanak chose to provide a fresh plurality and thus a new identity for spiritual upliftment and social welfare at the same time, when most of his contemporaries preached only other worldliness. But the controversy we often witness not only in India but in Europe and the USA as well, on small matters of ethnic distinctions such as the dress codes and food habits of his Sikh followers are not comparatively speaking vital issues of religious diversity. Thus the insistence on the use of turban by Sikh soldiers in the British Army or the insistence of certain Sikh organizati ons in India that women pillion riders on motor-cycles shall not wear safety helmets cannot be taken as core issues of religious faith as such demands are more of identity markers than spiritual practices. One could take similar examples from Islamic and Christian fold, such as wearing of large Crosses by Christians or head scarfs or skull-caps that loudly declare the religious affiliations of a person more than his/her inner conduct. This show of plurality is made up of mere diversity of dress codes or marriage customs. It does not ensure any deeper perceptions about the nature of reality and truth as they are defined for a better life according to the religious tenets of an adherent.

Teaching the Diversity of Faiths

The obligations of societies professing pluralism go beyond mere tolerance of external markers. Such societies are obliged to actively cultivate a reasonable acquaintance with the articles of divergent faiths and beliefs. But in most national systems of formal education world over, and particularly in the Indian one that inherits the British perspective, religious and moral education has been kept out of school and college education as a guiding principle of the secular state. For example in Indian educational system it is presumed that acquainting a Muslim child with Hindu precepts will obstruct his allegiance to his family faith and similarly teaching the basic tenets of Islam to a Hindu child will ruin his or her faith in tenets of parental Hinduism.

Hence, India like many a modern Western or Asian democratic non theocratic state prefers not to teach the precepts of different religions, and especially not even of her majority religion of Hinduism to her own school children lest this kind of teaching shake the faith of the children in their parental interpretation of religion. The Indian policy makers are further afraid if religious instruction is given, the State may be accused of promoting one religion over another or of even pushing religious values over and above the so called atheistic/agnostic/secular values of life that for some reason have acquired the aura of being more liberal, democratic and modern than religious ethics. In other words, it is presumed that knowing about the faith of others, and of the majority Hindu adherents of the nation in special, is detrimental to the security and freedom of a child's beliefs.

In India, another irrational fear has been practiced now for more than half a century ever since it was enshrined in the Constitution as an unwarranted phobia. Teaching of religion may end up as teaching of the majority religion, that is Hinduism and this may result in a religious oppression of religious minorities like the Muslims, Christians, Buddhists, Sikhs and atheists. Therefore, these minorities are not only 'protected' by the lack of religious education, they are given a Constitutional concession to open and manage religious or other institutions where freedom to teach their particular faith is guaranteed. In other words, a minority child is likely to be harmed by exposure to the faith of the majority and hence no general religious instruction in state schools, but a majority child is not likely to be harmed if he/she attends a minority school class in a minority institution. This theory of education is based on phobia and exclusion and instills a suspicion of faiths other than one is born into. Such a kinky pedagogy can only breed intolerant and ignorant members in a society who to satisfy their religious thirst can fall prey to any unhealthy cult ranging from aggressive dogmas to terrorism promoted from within or outside the nation.

Family, not an Efficient Teaching Space

One often hears the prescription that religion and its values are best taught by the family and the State far from having an obligation for providing education about religious matters should keep even the public media, such as news prints, television and public utility spaces sanitized from religious overtones. Besides promoting the tyranny of the Euro-centric post Enlightenment secularity, this notion simply overlooks (or secretly galore in) the fact that the family is no longer capable of giving proper religious instruction of even the faith it professes and least of all of the faiths of others. As a matter of fact most families, even the well-versed ones in religious concepts have a sectarian idea and irrational emotional attachment to their faith. They teach hostility and prejudice to other faiths. In fact, it is the prejudice instilled by families that pours into the public space as strife and the more deprived the public education about religious matters, greater the chances of conflict.

If plurality is to be promoted then a new public space for religious dialogue must be created. Seminars and conventions that are being so frantically arranged now all over the world cannot resolve prejudices that families have instilled for generations. The family is not expected to have a pluralistic and wide vision approach to religion that instruction in public spaces needs to evolve for a better world.

Older societies had chosen to demarcate social norms for adherents of divergent faiths in stricter terms. But people were more aware of the fundamentals of each other's religion or sect. For instance in ancient India, a Jain child may not have gone to the same educational institution (*ashrama*) along with a Buddhist or a Vaishnava child, or may have never shared lunch with a child that came from a family of the followers of Shiva, but the pedagogy of the times as practiced in schools of all denominations, had a rigorous system of teaching the precepts of other systems even though for the purpose of refutation. In other words, a Jain child or a mature scholar would surely know the precepts of all other sects. And so would a Buddhist or a Shaivite scholar. But what is taught nowadays in schools and universities the world over is not the way to distinguish between the why and how of different faiths but a namby-pamby multi-culturalism constantly reeling under the weight or some ideology, usually western, be it neo-colonialism, senile socialism or a carpet-bagger globalization.

In pre-technocratic cultures spaces of common activities were fewer than now in the present age of high mobility and intermixing. In the face of the great uniformization that occurs through mass production, perhaps religion, language, skin-color, marital laws and food are the few markers left with us today for making group distinctions amongst vast populations. The last two, that is, marital laws and food, may not be distinct for very long and may become uniform in another half a century. A hybrid global cuisine of the fast food variety and serial monogamy of the Christian heritage is already the emerging trend. Therefore, it is all the more essential that an informed and open-minded view is cultivated about religion, skin-color, and language by people the world over. But in order to secure some degree of success in this direction, we must shift the emphasis from harping upon the differences between peoples, races, religions, and cultures to the deeper unity of humankind.

Distorted Notions of Secularity

One of the biggest hurdles in the modern times regarding religious education is the distorted notion of secularity that demands a total separation of the Church (not just Christian Church but the organized or semi-morphic body representing any religion) from the State to maintain an equal distance from all religious denominations. The events of the European Reformation and its aftermath in which the material power of the Christian Church was reduced, still hang heavy as a collective memory in social orders that have inherited this civilization. This fear has made the education systems in the West (and as much in the East where the colonial models were followed) totally divorced from religious heritage and very often valueless and hollow. And this is particularly so because the so called Humanism of the Enlightenment has proved to be too anthropocentric and consumerist. The Marxist animosity to religion viewed as 'opium of the masses' is another major factor that contributes to the banning of religious notions from educational systems. Ethics thus is the biggest casualty of civilization today.

It is high time that the modern state should redefine its secularity which can no longer mean atheism, agnosticism or theophobia but an active engagement in imparting the basic tenets of all faiths in the world and specifically so that are professed by its majority and minority populations of each land. And this should be done not as a concession but as an endeavor that answers the deepest aspirations of mankind and makes it harmonious with other beings and non-beings on the planet. I may add here that the ideal before the Indian State, namely what has been carefully defined in India as '*sarva-dharma-sambhaava*' (equal regard for all faiths) endeavors in this direction. It may be noted that in the Indian philosophical systems as in the common psyche of its people even atheism or even the Marxist materialistic dialecticism is just one another faith (*matam/ sampradaaya*), that is a set of metaphysical, existential and ethical notions that sustain its adherents. Hence the divide between a secular and a godly system of faith does not exist as the state is committed to the well being of the adherents of all systems. It is then its bounden duty to educate its children and grown ups in all the faiths so that not only they fulfill their denominational needs but learn to understand the faiths of others. Perhaps a rigorous pursuit of this path shall prevent us from frantically trying to dole out palliatives in emergencies as has been the case regarding Islam after 9/ 11.

An Example of Faith Diversity Curriculum

I have had personally the opportunity to be involved in some policy-making exercises regarding religious education in India. Although most of this has remained at the level of planning and is far from execution due to lack of political consensus, a fresh thinking about the content of modern education, particularly at the school level is already underway in India. One such long exercise was conducted in 2002 at the Indira Gandhi National Center for the Arts, New Delhi by a committee of educational experts and then in office chairperson of the National Women's Commission. I had the opportunity to lead the committee as the Convener.

It was felt by us that religious plurality cannot be introduced into a school curriculum as mere verbal statements of the articles of diverse faiths to be memorized by pupils. That would be just another kind of catechism. Introducing the religious concepts should be part of the larger plan to make the young acquainted with their cultural and scientific heritage of India as a whole. Religions can make sense when they are taught in relation to architecture, dance, music, painting, poetry, drama, history and mythology, traditional medicine and knowledge systems preserved by the forest and mountain peoples. The documented part of religious texts, the so-called scriptures make much more meaning in relation to other forms of religious expression that depends upon music, poetry and so many arts. As a method of collecting the advice of the schools, a series of conferences and workshops were held in each of which teachers and principals of about 50 schools were invited to offer their views. Much care was taken to invite teachers from the Christian and Muslim schools as well besides the regular schools of Hindu majority. We found that there was a great enthusiasm about changing the print oriented and examination modelled system of teaching and grading and nearly all the proposals tended to demand a system in which learning would be provided through a greater involvement of the arts. It was repeatedly mentioned that the much needed communication skills could be easily acquired through various arts and particularly through theatre for the children.

To begin with it was emphasized that the diversified nature of Indian society as a unique mosaic of traditions and cultures, ranging from hunting-gathering communities like the primitive Jarawas of the Andaman and Nicobar Islands to the most complex urban cultures of its cosmopolitan towns must be made familiar to students. The present school system was too centralized, elite-dominated and urban-oriented. It will have to undergo several modifications to relate itself to the needs and convenience of various communities and young learners, if India is to have a strong base of Heritage Education (HE). The new cultural curriculum and pedagogy must take into account the life-views and living styles of the communities to which the school going children belong and adapt the content of learning to their needs and aspirations. Severe neglect of the sense of belonging to the community makes the present day system of schooling uninteresting and even unacceptable to many. After exhaustive discussions following conclusions were drawn:

(1) Cultural Heritage studies should be named as Heritage Activity. The change in name was made to emphasize that 'culture' very often stays limited to the fine arts and that students should not be asked to memorize certain facts about 'culture' but to feel the place of culture in the broad ambience of the total heritage that includes religion, science, history and ethics in a tangible way through practical activities to be prescribed for the classes. Culture is not an isolated activity but as a whole vision of life.

(2) The Heritage Activity shall NOT be made as extra curricular but shall be evaluated and marked as other curricular subjects. It shall be taught in all classes in

the school curriculum right from primary classes till the last class of the school.

(3) The children are needed to be encouraged to develop a more of a play-like atmosphere in tuning themselves to HA and entirely so in the lower classes through music, painting, theatre, recitation, and such arts. There should be a gradual transition from the experiential in the lower classes to the conceptual in higher classes. At all levels students shall be involved practically in learning about the material heritage (such as archaeological sites, temples, museums etc.,) and abstract heritage (philosophies, poetry, scriptures) forms of Indian Heritage through work-books, projects and visits to sites and less through textbooks.

(4) The instructional materials of various subjects shall be divided into practical and conceptual modes of instructions but shall be transmitted through projects and activities.

(5) Besides the school system, other cultural resource centers such as museums, historical sites, documentation centers, research institutions, places of worship, holy sites, pilgrimages etc., shall be visited to feel a closeness and respect for the living heritage and the various regions of India.

(6) In order to provide room for heritage activity and not impose additional work load on students, obsolete and repetitive content from the various existing subjects, can be shed after proper scrutiny.

(7) Training should be given to the present teachers to teach the Heritage Activity. Teachers from diverse

existing subjects can very well teach HA after training. HA need not require additional hiring of teachers.

(8) Special care shall be taken to use the local, regional and geographical aspects of Heritage around the school to accommodate the diversity of Indian culture. The HA work-books and projects shall be prepared at state levels and also reflects some national elements.

(9) The curriculum should also be made to reflect and highlight the living urban and folk wisdom of the traditions of India.

Following themes are identified as constituting the essential aspects of India's Heritage.

a) Sacred sites and architectural heritage.

b) Folklore and lifestyles of Rural, Tribal and Urban India.

c) Visual, Oral, Performing and Fine Arts of India.

d) Scriptural Heritage of India, including all religious and cultural texts.

e) Literature and Literary Figures of India.

f) Philosophers, Thinkers and Saints.

g) Traditional Modes of Transmission of History, Arts and Culture.

It is needless to say that the detailed syllabi for projects, cultural activity, work-books, community activity, teaching of arts and crafts etc., is a task to be undertaken by experts of various heritage subjects from early to highest class according to the suggestions and guidelines given above, should the policy makers ever decide to implement this vision of pluralism in religious and cultural education.

Curricula for Plurality Needed in Europe and America

What has been proposed for the Indian situation above need not be treated as applicable to India alone but can be used by various countries. It is a model of treating plurality that exists in many cultures. The 20th century has already witnessed a vast migration of Arabs and Asians into Europe, North America and Australia. The trend is likely to intensify and create highly diverse societies in these continents. Muslims, Sikhs, Hindus and Orthodox Christians are now a permanent part of these regions. For this reason the Indian conditions and the suggested model preserving harmonious diversity can of great use to some major nations like the USA, Canada, UK and the EU that are now grappling with racial, linguistic, and ethnic conflicts. The ignorance of the Christians about Hinduism and its diverse faith is simply appalling as one notes from the many incidents of Sikhs being mistaken as followers of Osama and shot in the USA. One may observe, though, that whereas in India much wider and intense diversity has existed for many millennia, it is relatively new in these continents and therefore even its smaller scale may be more difficult to deal with. Particularly so when Christianity and Islam both preach the doctrine of the elect and the fundamental right to proselytize that stands in the way of harmony and mutual admiration of faiths.

It is my hope that an educational policy that is able to open up the young minds to religious diversity shall also result in locating a common ground between various religious and cultural beliefs. It may be remembered that commonality between beliefs and not their differences are the *raison d'etre* of communication. If communication is to be something more than exchange of goods or info-commodity, then we may benefit most from turning to the core of vibrant similarity between religions and cultural identities that exists beneath all differences and which, instead of being wiped out by the individual differences, sustains itself and the differences as well. To provide a simile, it is like the consonance between two musical notes, which are always independent but are always capable of generating a mutual resonance by virtue of their common grounding in a given scale. Within our pluralism we need to explore our common scale.

Today one cannot escape dealing with the theme of religious and cultural diversity in the context of globalization that demands harmonious interchange between cultures and nations. Hence for a peaceful growth of the global interchanges a strong mutual appreciation of religious tenets is essential. Religion happens to be one source of causing a lot of misunderstanding among the diverse peoples of the world as they mostly do not understand the approaches of those who follow a different faith from theirs. This problem needs to be overcome as early as possible. This task of building understanding of others' faith cannot be left to voluntary good doers or whosoever claims to address it but should be the part of the education system from childhood onwards. As at initial levels almost entirely, and at higher levels partially, managing the educational system is essentially the duty of the State, governments world over should adopt a pluralistic approach to religion in making it a part of education.

Part Three

PRITHVI : Diminishing Boundaries

18

Indian Diaspora

The Brihad Bharat

At the very start of the 21st Century, not only the demise of Socialism but also the inadequacy of Consumerist Globalism is becoming increasingly evident. Most Western strategists portray the conflict scenario as a cultural clash, a well known model being that of Samuel Huntington. His strategy was basically to create a West versus the Rest paradigm which one way or another, promotes a non-democratic hegemony of the Euro-American. Hence his portraiture of Islam as a consolidated force and that of India as a "lonely Hindu nation" without a strong diasporic support dependent for its survival on American goodwill. Barely two years after a lecture by Huntington expressing the above sentiments delivered at the Rajiv Gandhi Foundation (Feb1998), India demolished not only the myth of her loneliness by showing the world its expanding nuclear power and the success of its diaspora. Far from a lonely nation, India is being recognised and sought after as a vast repository of skilled labour and investment opportunities.

The Changed Order of the 21st Century

The 19th century migration of indentured labour from India was meant to fill the gap created by the abolishment of slavery in the British colonies of Africa, Pacific and South America. But in the mid 20th century, Indian migration to Europe and North America took a new turn. A fresh generation of professionals and semi-professionals entered the technological and medical streams in Europe and North America and achieved many eminent and enviable positions. This change made the Indiaspora, though only 0.5% of the total American population, a socially visible group that can influence public life, to some degree. It is not a temporary but a permanent change. The educated high degree holders continue to make their places not out of mere financial need but more from the strong desire to carve a place of eminence in the technocratic societies of the world and serve India from adopted lands. What was once called the brain drain has proved to be a brain implant.

The Closet-Cultured Diaspora of Nehruvian Era

Before the Independence there was an expectation fom the diasporic or expatriate Indians to speak forth strongly and even work for the Freedom Struggle. But in the fifties under the approach to the international affairs as forstered by Nehru, the diaspora was advised to be a quiet law abiding mass that should be politically voiceless, faithfully following the established norms of the adopted societies. India was supposed to be too weak till the sixties to even protest against the displacement of its people in Africa or to speak against the policy of the Melting Pot in America. The diaspora was in any case too insecure to think beyond making the two ends meet. As a result, a whole generation adopted a schizophrenic life-style in which the public space was oppressively alien and the private home stagnantly native.

Culture was relegated to a cupboard status feeding on nostalgia and heirlooms. The gap between the adopted country and the home country was very wide.

Nationality, now less Topographic, more Emotional

In the so called new world order, the concept of nationality has undergone a sea change. With the emergence of the European Union, nationalism has been redefined not only for the nation states of Europe but even for the people of Asian and African continents. In the very Euro-American societies that developed the concept of nationalism, the construct of ethnicity has come to almost replace the basic building block of nationalism. We have a situation in which borders may be defined by the older nationalism, while the social fabric is divided into 'ethnic', categories. Every nation is therefore, seen as multi-ethnic conglomerate. With this devaluation of the nationhood and the privileging of ethnicity, the new communication technology is making the cultural-ethnic bonds so strong that expatriate populations can now live in a close emotional proximity to the native land though physically on the other side of the globe. The emotional bonds are easier to maintain in the age of internet, tv, emails, faxes and phones than in the earlier age of letters and newspapers. In this new scenario, it all depends upon the Indian state, whether it is able to reawaken the emotional links of Indiaspora or continue with the Nehruvian apathy. I hope that the newly formed Ministry for diaspora will take major steps in this direction which are better thought out than the erstwhile "Festival of India" fiascos.

The Government of India and the Indian people have now to stand up to the challenge of providing cultural support to its diaspora in an unprecedented way. If they merely look upon them as bankers, investors and creditors, it shall be a grevious pitfall. We have already started to reduce them into economic milch cows. If the relationship is merely economic it shall not be an enduring one. Markets are not upbeat all the time. Besides it does not give Indian diaspora a special status different from investors and creditors of other nationalities.

Indiasporas: of Africa, Far East, Gulf and Euro-American Space

The Indian State policy of relating to the diaspora has not been need specific but only a vague treatment of them all as nostalgic expatriates. The kind of equations that African Indiaspora needs to establish with the motherland is very different from that required by the East Asian or American Indiasporians. Once the GOI has located their specific needs, the various State Governents in India will need to act differently also involving the state NGOs. Everything should not be left to the Centre as this tends to create too generalised solutions that reduce effictiveness. States like Punjab, Kerala, Gujarat and Tamil Nadu need to make special efforts as people from these regions have a major presence abroad. The States can benefit most from their ex-citizens in the field of education who can help revive many institutions from schools to Universities. The diasporians themselves have a lot to gain from better educational centres for sake of their own children. Seeing the pitiable conditions of Universities in Gujarat, I have always wondered why no money has never been invested by the billionaire expatriates. The same applies to Kerala. The kind of pride that diasporians feel in their regional identities can be made more meaningful if specific projects of cultural involvement are realised. The number of institutions aided or managed in India by the PIO (persons of Indian origin) living abroad is, at present, much too small. It tends to benefit middle-class professions and not the village level youth who are in dire need of training for blue collar jobs.

Resistance to New Slavery : Pull vs Push

The movement of the skilled Indians to other lands has barely begun to gather momentum. As the number of educated unemployed Indians continues to rise, the Push to move shall mount. But so will the Pull from post-industrial societies of Europe and America as the labouring age-group is declinig in the local populations. But the Cyber-Rush can be as dehumanising as was the Gold-Rush of the Wild West, if adequate protections are not sought for the people through new nondiscriminatory and humanitarian immigration laws of the receiving countries. The GOI must take this task seriously and ask for safeguards through diplomatic channels and global forums. One can clearly see a backlash in the offing against migrants and steps to handle must be worked out in advance. In the Gulf region, the treatment meted out to Indians is already in contravention of human rights. The custody of passport with the employer, restrictions on communications, near inhuman behaviour with women working as house-help, are some of the issues that need to be taken up internationally without fear of souring diplomatic ties with Gulf nations.

Establishing Indian Heritage in Global Space

The Indiaspora needs to be convinced that in order to survive as independent people in the adopted lands they need to grow with their heritage not just merely cling to it. Apart from many strategies for hightening their security-comfort, they need to intervene in the educational systems of adopted lands. So far only parallel tracks of cultural visibility such as temples and gurdwaras have been established. But the real dialogue with the inhabitants of land can come after some room has been made in the curriculum for Indian philosophies and cultural beliefs. This is going to be a major task that calls for persistant and planned effort using the latest technologies for a long time.

Atman : The Self in Doubt

An Indian philosopher residing in Persia accompanied some ayurvedic doctors in the Persian armies of Darius invading Greece in 492 BC But before the battle of Marathon, he disappeared into the country side. A decade later, he came to settle in Athens, disputing and debating in the agora and came to be popularly known as "Pharatos." After his death, he entered the Elysian Fields; from where like other philosophers and learned souls in Hades, he continues to look at the global human affairs from his times to the present, as an unexamined life is not worth living even after death.

We give, here, two dialogues of Pharatos, "Relativism: A Moral Twilight" and "Searching for the Sahaj".

19

Relativism
A Moral Twilight

It was under the big platanos tree in the center of Elysian orchards that Pharatos usually sat waiting for Socrates to finish his walk and join him.

"I never thought it was going to be any better in the Fortune Islands as all this company may never be able to enter them. You know, one has to take three rebirths and lead three virtuous lives to come to Elysium before one gets to those immortal islands. If all our company that sits under this tree is unable to make it to the islands, I shall not be happy listening to the songs of Homer alone."

"Indeed there are new dangers now in living in the upper world," said Socrates. But Kokkinophoros exclaimed, "Why so, it seems a safer place, you don't die of fever so quickly or from snake bite. This new allopathic medicine saves so many lives. Aisklepios could not have dreamt of such success. Had the population on the earth not increased, there would be fewer arrivals from Styx and the dog Kerberos would have gone lazy. He would have hardly any sneakers to catch."

"But people are still dying in huge numbers in spite of allopathic surgery and drugs," said Pharatos. "Allopathy can't cure a simple thing like a headache, what to talk of mass killers like diabetes, fatness, stones in bladder, thrombosis and what not. Allopathy treats the body like a chariot, it replaces the worn out part. But it cannot revitalize any part. If one of your horses is old or weak it can put a new one in its place. Whereas Asklepios or Charaka treated the body as a tree and with better food, water, air or earth made the sap flow again to bring new leaves. But the science of Asklepios is gone in Hellas and survives poorly in India as 'Unani'. It is disregarded as much as ancient Indian medical science called the Ayurveda by the Indian Health Ministry which, as a newly famous yoga guru Ramdev says, should be called Allopathy Ministry."

Before Kokkinophoros, the ever red with rage, could say anything, Socrates intervened, "Is it not more important to note that nowadays the world has a much sicklier psyche in the taller and bigger bodies that they sport? You may debate about what kind of medicine is best but I do not know how these moderns cure their minds even if they succeed in maintaining their tougher frames. They are sitting on a nuclear dump and are yet fighting, so much and so often."

"Quite so, Socrates," said Pharatos. "It is not just the danger of war, but the dangerous life in peace that seems to be the biggest puzzle. With so much wealth, there is so little happiness, song, music, dance and dialogue, that this modernity seems poorer in the mind and spirit than any age before."

Socrates again interjected, "As I was saying all the time in the Athenian agora that when democracy starts decaying, the ruling classes are most known by their inability to take decisions. It is a kind of ethical paralysis that sets in and slowly brings the whole edifice of Law to the ground. Rulers can make the state survive with little riches if they take right decisions at the right time, but the state may not last if rulers are unable to decide on things. Themistokles decided to make the big fleet for securing the power of Athens in the seas and hence Athenians were able to defeat the Persians at Salamis but when the Athenians could not control their wasteful and repeated use of navy against Sparta in the 27 year war, they lost the city to Spartans. Democracy, when overdone, brings not just wrong decisions, but the sterility to take them at all. Don't you see this happening in India right now? They can't even decide whether or not to move the cows away from the streets of Delhi. What to talk of how to stop Islamic terrorists that keep attacking the people of the city."

"Is this inability to take decisions caused by the decay of democracy alone where the council of ministers often consists of men of poor education and even under-trials for all sorts of crimes?" asked Xenophon. More than democratic decay, influential behavior in the world is governed today by a philosophy of amoralism or meta-ethics. They think one man's meat is another man's poison so nothing is good or bad in itself. It is good for the cow to live on the road but bad for the man whose garden she eats."

Socrates said triumphantly, "But don't you agree Pharatos that a soft democracy, as we see today in the land of your origin, has many rulers with the brains of a cow. They can't even think for the well being of a cow let alone of a human. So leaving aside the influence of dogmas like Relativism, democracy done poorly is enough for the ruin of a people."

"I know your suspicions about democracy, Socrates," said Pharatos, "and share them entirely but the philosophy of amoralism seems to be infesting the European and the American lands much more. Indians don't seem to espouse that doctrine so often. Instead of making fine points about the basis of a moral choice they are either plain corrupt or opportunistic."

Kokkinophoros, who had stayed quiet for too long, could not help observing, "All right, Pharatos, as you belong, or rather belonged to India, before coming over to Hellas with Persian armies and spending the rest of your life in Athens, tell us why are your country men so adept in using different ethical rules on different occasions that they are now excelling the Europeans in moral relativism? What has happened to the idea of righteous action or *dharma* as you call it? Are there many *dharmas* and can different people follow them differently as we see it being done now? How is that distinct from the dogma of relativism or amoralism?"

Calming him down Socrates said, "Be not so red with excitement, Kokkinophoros! There can be only one Good not many. If there are many *dharmas* for many people then no Good can come out of them for the people. True, if diverse people have diverse *dharmas*, then *dharma* cannot be distinct from relativism so fashionable today? *Dharma* in that case is no better than a puzzle, a peep into chaos, an aporia, and a moral relativism. Has it always not been this way in India? And is that not the reason for the elite classes to have fallen into somnambulism these days in accordance with their age-old habit? Or do you differ, Pharatos?"

"*Dharma*, Socrates, is not obedience to a set of rules," began Pharatos on a longer exposition, "Nor is *dharma* just a code of conduct even though you have been hearing the Indian pundits expound on so many precepts that are finally summed up by saying '*dharmo eshah sanaatanah*', "this is the eternal *dharma.*" With such a position the possibility of an Indian belief in moral relativism is simply set aside. If there is an eternal *dharma* how can there be any relativism? Does relativism not preach that there are many different moralities or moral norms and all are equally good? One may practice any of them according to the country one is born into. Is "that not correct?"

"Yes, indeed," agreed Socrates.

"Then having set aside any shade of moral relativism from Indian thought let us explore why there can be so many ways of acting and yet all of them can be just and leading to *dharma*. Tell me; are you not all familiar with the duty of the protector of a supplicant that may bring him or her into conflict with one's own kith and kin? Or, why is it, that having made an oath, a man is often compelled to do what he would not submit to, in normal conditions? When Oedipos vowed to banish the sinner whose sin had brought the plague to Thebes, could he have gone back on his word for the sake of his children, when it was discovered that he himself was the sinner? Or to take an example from the Indian epic *Mahabharata* this, could Karna, the great warrior, after he discovered that he was the eldest of the Pandava heroes, have gone back on his vow to kill them in the great battle in the plains of Kurukshetra? Can you say then, that one is free to choose a value different from the one espoused at the time of embarking on a course of action?"

"A minute ago, Pharatos, you said that *dharma* was not just obedience to the rule and now you say that one must live to the precept of keeping an oath?" asked Kokkinophoros. "If rules of conduct are to be followed for the sake of duty, is that not *dharma*? Or do you still insist *dharma* is something else, Pharatos?"

"That, indeed, is the loose definition of *dharma*. But following the correct code of conduct is better called '*aachaara*' not *dharma*. There are times, when for the sake of *dharma*, one has to follow an unheard or unusual course which may seem unwise or even wrong to the established opinion or the common folks."

You mean, for instance, the conduct of Gandhi in sleeping besides young girls to test the chastity of his mind?" asked an amused Kokkinophoros.

"No, no that was an unnecessary demonstration of Gandhi's vanity. Who can know the purity of a person's mind except the person himself? Such things can never be proved to anybody else. Besides, if he was serious, Gandhi should have slept next to some formidable temptress rather than frightened little girls," said Pharatos. "What I mean is illustrated by the example of a celibate monk carrying a drowning young woman in his arms across the river to help her reach her home, or the case of a hermit speaking untruth to mislead a hunter to save the life of a pregnant deer."

He went on at length saying, "The rules of conduct are not *dharma* but choosing between the different courses of action in a crisis and deciding on the right path is *dharma*. It is the knowledge of the self and the duty at the moment in the interest of not one but all. *Dharma*, thus, is to know the right course of action. Rules of conduct or *aacharana* can be rejected or modified according to time and place and yet be enhancing the *sanatana* or the eternal *dharma*. Conduct changes with times and there can be no moral rules good for all times and all places. In the available writings of orthodox Islam, all the actions of the Prophet Muhammad, peace be upon him, are beyond any evaluation. In the traditional Islamic view, his life is an example that must be emulated by a pious Muslim and all kinds of explanations are available for his each and every conduct. It is clear that none of his actions is held as valid for his times alone."

"On the contrary, in the Hindu tradition, the example of a particular conduct of the Rama, the Divine in an earthly incarnation, does not make it automatically correct for a present day Hindu. Given the belief that as an incarnation or *avatara* when the Divine takes up the human form, recognizable human fallibilities become part of his conduct, no *avatara* can be an example of conduct to be followed for all times. Not only have the Hindus been discussing the frailties of their *avataras*, they have even been joking about it. These frailties are recognized as part of the essential nature of an imperfect universe or even of the godhood that incarnates as an imperfect human being."

"So should we say, Pharatos, that *dharma* is not the conduct of an individual but is the consequence of his conduct or praxis?" inquired Xenophon.

"Yes, it could be put this way. Conduct, in the Indian systems, not just Hindu, but in all indigenous Indian systems, is divided into *dharma* and *aachaara*. *Dharma* is that which sustains an individual, a family, a country or the immutable self, the *Atma,* and is achieved by the right *aachaara* or praxis. *Dharma* for an individual may sometimes conflict with his habits or with what is thought to be his family *dharma.* In such a dilemma (*dharma-sankata*) the choice to be made may be different for different persons. The choice, the action, the *aachaara,* must vary according to the situation of the doer. Karna, the hero in *Mahabharata*, had sworn to fight for his friend Duryodhana and fulfil the duty to the friend (*sakhaa-dharma*). Hence he could not fulfil his duty as a son (*putra-dharma*) in obeying his mother Kunti who asked him not to fight a mortal combat with his brother Arjuna in the battle. But he promised to spare his other four brothers which his vow and the loyalty to the friend, *sakhaa-dharma,* allowed. But he did not give up duty to his friend (*sakhaa-dharma*) to please his mother in spite of the impending and sure death waiting for him as a result of his choice. It may be argued that had he chosen to obey his mother and crossed over to the other side, the war would have come to an earlier end and he would have saved many thousands of lives. A modern pacifist, or specially a post-modernist relativist, or a smart sub-alternist would perhaps extol such a choice. But in the classical scheme of things, the hero Karna would have lost his word, and would have been accused of being a self-seeker who violated allegiance for the petty gain of his life."

Pharatos paused to see the impact of his argument on the company. While Socrates and Xenophon seemed to be chewing over the idea, the chronic opponent Kokkinophoros shot back. "I do not see what could have been wrong in Karna choosing to change sides, seeing that he would have supported the cause of peace and just men like his five brothers, the Pandavas? Moral relativism does not mean selfishness. Why not choose the cause of peace."

"Peace or convenience? Why did Orestes not conveniently stay quiet but instead killed his mother Klytemnestra, the killer of his father? He would have been spared the wrath of the furies for committing the sin of killing a mother."

"But tell me Pharatos," asked Socrates, "are you saying that one should not change the course of one's action just because one has taken a vow, given a word, even though one may discover that he is on the side that is wrong? Is keeping one's word the supreme *dharma*, an end in itself? If I discover a relatively better option that is in the general good, can I not change the course of action, *aachaara* as you call it?"

"The vow, Socrates, is merely the culmination of a path chosen, presumably not in passion but in deep understanding. For Karna, prince Duryodhana was not only a benefactor but also the man who gave him the status of the great hero which he deserved but which was denied to him by the rest of the world, and by his royal mother no less, because he was made by her into a foundling growing in the home of low born parents. Karna was loyal to those who raised him in love and he rightly denied the mere claim of blood."

"Let us take another paradigm, this time from the older Indian epic the Ramayana, the case of Vibhishana, the blood brother of the tyrant Raavana. Vibhishana had no obligation to obey his elder brother Raavana as he was not bound to Raavana, even though a brother, because he did not practice the life style and values of Raavana. Vibhishana chose not to support Raavana right from the start of the conflict with prince Rama. He acted for the larger good of his city Lanka, his land of birth. Here his *aachaara* reflected the larger good. Between the duty to the family (*kula-dharma*) and duty to the city (*raashtra-dharma*) he chose the latter."

"However no historical example, is totally valid for copying. Examples are valid for discussion and interpretation only as all individuals acted according to the *dharma* relevant to their times. The praxis of a present day person should be based on the values and situations dictated by the present."

"Regarding the ancient characters or examples we cannot insist that there is only one exact/historical/objective version of the life as lived by a person or character. There can be many accounts of a given life. Such are the limitations of recording and transmitting history that many versions can co-exist and be relevant. In their exasperation, the natural sciences-fed-historians would call such an approach as diversion from history and surrender to mythology."

"Pharatos, you seem to be attached to the position of persons who wrote the narratives in which the heroes were acting according to the notions of what is just or *dharma* as seen by the narrator. What about a different position? Such as a pacifist's position?" asked Xenophon.

"I am familiar with the thinking of many intellectuals who espouse pluralism and relative ethical positions to judge a text," replied Pharatos. But tell me, Xenophon, can anybody other than the creator of a text has the right to unmake the narrative and the moral universe of that narration. If we believe that this world has laws different from those given in a story by the maker, we should write our own instead of imposing our systems on somebody's story. Tell me where does pacifism work with a person like Raavana, Duryodhana or let us say Hitler, Stalin, Mao or a Jehaadi warrior? You can write the story of how the Buddha transformed a heinous murderer. But such narratives are very normative and hypothetical and hence contrived. In real life there is no escape from the battle field."

"You are saying, what we the ancient Greeks believed... Peace, comforting and beautiful as it may be, is only an interlude between the ever present reality of war," chimed in Kokkinophoros.

As the time for the siesta approached and the sunshine made the company drowsy, Socrates stood up and others also. They started on their diverse ways to the shades of their favorite trees, away from the big platanos that soon left by itself waived gently in the breeze.

****

A note on the Greek Underworld:

1. It has an entrance by the Okeanos stream having on its sides the black poplars.
2. The dead spirits pay a coin (which is placed in funeral rites under corpse's tongue) to be given Charon to cross Styx, the western boundary of Tartarus, which has six tributary rivers including the one called Lethe. The ghosts of the dead without a coin wait endlessly on the banks of the Styx or evade Hermes and enter through a back entrance.
3. The arrival shore of Styx is guarded by the fierce dog called Kerberos.
4. In the Underworld, Tartarus begins with depressing Asphodel Fields where heroes and common folks twitter alike. The only joys available to them are the libations of blood poured for them in ancestral rites by their relatives.

5. Tartarus has Erebus and the mansions of Hades and Persephone. The commoners here drink from the waters of the river Lethe and forget their lives but the wise drink from the waters of Memory.

6. Three judges judge the dead spirits. Radamanthys examines the cases of Asians, Aecus of Europeans and Minos takes up the difficult ones.

7. The average people go to Asphodel fields, the evil-doers to the punishment-fields and the virtuous to orchards of Elysium.

8. Elysium has the river of Memory. It is always day there, it is neither cold nor it snows. Always going on are games and music. The inhabitants of Elysium can chose rebirth and after three Elysium entries and then can go forever to the Fortunate Islands. (based on *Greek Myths* by Robert Graves).

****

20

Searching for the Sahaj
In Pursuit of Abiding Happiness

It was a bright day after the morning shower in Elysium, when Pharatos was reclining under the platanos tree waiting for the philosophers. They arrived leisurely, their faces lit by the touch of the pleasant air that was so different after several days of dryness bearing now the smells of orchard fruits. Truly, the faraway twittering of the unwise in the Asphodel fields could hardly be heard today.

"I am curious," said Socrates, "why just a little change in weather makes a man happy or depressed although equanimity is the best course for the thoughtful?" Why is it natural for human beings, indeed for all living creatures, to seek pleasure and avoid pain? Even here in the Underworld!!"

"I do not think that there can be a question that this is the way things are and always going to be," observed Aristotle. "The more important thing is to understand where does true happiness lie and how can humans pursue it."

It was now the turn of the ever-scoffing Kokkinophoros to interject. "If all beings go after pleasure and shun pain, and such is the order of the world, the best course in life would be to collectively ensure security and safety and see that no group of persons exploits others. Of course, there has to be a class of guardians that ensures the existence and preservation of such a social order. We have had such a city state, at least for some time, in Sparta."

"You are presuming here that a secure state is condition enough for happiness," said Socrates. "The state often represses individual happiness while it may provide safety from other predatory states."

"And what we have now seen for more than two thousand years sitting here in the lower world is that in human affairs the guardians very soon turn into tyrants themselves and thus the state crumbles under their own corruption and lust for power," added Socrates. "We have to analyze how to find happiness for every single person. We have many answers, such as the notion of eudaimonia as pointed out by Aristotle, which is not just some hours of intermittent pleasure, but activity that is virtuously done without interruption."

At this point Pharatos asked the company if there could ever be a possibility of unimpeded pleasure, no matter how virtuous the course of action might be. The notion of what is virtuous is different to different persons in diverse times and places, he added. Furthermore, some of our most virtuous actions sometimes bring very painful results.

"Tell me, Aristotle, if there is any unmixed pleasure in actual experience in everyday life. Perhaps it is to be found only in art. The artist gives an imitative representation of life. We get pleasure in seeing this imitation because, as you are fond of saying, Aristotle, imitation or mimesis is pleasant because it instructs and educates. And imitation in art is also joyful as it creates an impersonal feeling of universal emotion.

In life, all of us have a personal attraction, repulsion or unconcern to whatever person, object or event, we see. But in an artistic representation, say as in a tragedy, we do not react personally but with an impersonal emotion, which we enjoy. That is why in tragedy or art, we even enjoy emotions such as fear, sorrow and horror, which we shun in actual life. So unimpeded happiness is known as an aesthetic experience, and that too, only in art, but not in life."

"Look, Pharatos, I had defined eudaimonia as a culmination of the contemplative mind. The thinker does not look for self-gratification in every moment, but develops an attitude of calmness and takes pain in his stride, as much as he enjoys the pleasures that he encounters, during the course of his virtuous actions," explained Aristotle.

"But let me ask you, Aristotle," countered Pharatos, "what does this contemplative equanimity result in? Is it a state of pleasure unalloyed or is it a calmness that has come from the end of the threat of pain. Also, I want to know if eudaimonia is really *rising above* the cycle of pleasure and pain or is it a courageous but everlasting endurance of it? Perhaps you mean that it is pleasure proper to the contemplative activity, just as there exists pleasure proper to tragedy, the *oikeia hedone*?"

"You could say so," conceded Aristotle.

"In that case," Pharatos asserted, "the contemplative pleasure would also wear out, as you admit that all pleasures do sooner or later, and will leave a void in the heart of the individual for something more abiding and everlasting. We also have to admit that in spite of all contemplative fortitude, it is human nature to long for unalloyed pleasure. There are two ways of seeking this.

"One way is to do it by seeking a state of joy that is above the cycle of pleasure and pain in the world. It is the pursuit of an experiential state that has disengaged itself from running after pleasures, however refined or contemplative, and also from running away from pain though endured with the highest fortitude. It is a state of joy that a person arrives into, by neither longing for the pleasures of the body nor by mental stimulation nor by shunning physical or mental pain. It is a positive state of bliss that has transcended the everyday consciousness of the ego.

"The second way is to arrive at a state of vacuity, or the state of having neither joy nor depression nor any other feeling of exaltation or submission. It is a state of total openness in which the consciousness sees the flow of whatever is happening at the moment. It is a state of stillness or no-motion. Will you not grant that both these states, as I have described above, are different from eudaimonia of your description?"

"I would say so," said Aristotle. "What you are describing is not eudaimonia which does not call for this kind of transcendence of the ego. The eudaimonic man is, all said and done, a distinct individual or rather a very specially refined person."

"I am glad you admit as much, for that makes our task simpler, namely of pointing out that the pursuit of virtue by a refined man is nothing beyond social, moral and aesthetic excellence. It is not the case of a pursuant attaining a special state of being," said Pharatos.

"Eudaimonia is a special state indeed, because such an excellence is an uncommon achievement. It is not however a transcendental state, Pharatos," affirmed Aristotle.

At this point Socrates had to interject and he did so by saying that Pharatos was presuming that perfect happiness could not be achieved till the ego of the pursuant is transcended. "I appreciate that there will always a cause for unhappiness as long as the personal notions of an individual come into conflict with what is perceived as good or bad, favorable or hostile, but that dissolution of the ego and all notions of the virtuous or good, if abandoned, would mean that such a state of transcendental happiness is very personal and not socially useful," he added.

"But what harm is there, Socrates? All happiness is a personal experience, and in the state of bliss that I am describing, the experiencer, being a dispassionate person, is able to take a non-partisan stand on all social and worldly matters and thus can be termed as truly enlightened," said Pharatos rather emphatically.

"And what is the second way to happiness that you just talked about?" asked Kokkinophoros, "your second mystic option, if we may so call it."

"The second way, which calls for elimination of the ego or the self, is as much a transcendence of all pleasant and painful experiences of the body and the mental notions good and bad. However, those who talk about it do not say it is a bliss but they describe it only as stillness and quietitude," said Pharatos.

"Are these two states not called by the names of *ananda* and *nirvana* respectively?" asked Xenophon.

"Yes, indeed, you have caught on correctly, being the historian of philosophy that you are."

"If that is so, then why there has been, in your part of the world, so much of divergence for many millennia over these two traditions, that is, between the followers of *ananda* and the followers of *nirvana* or *kaivalya*? Both the states are affirming the road to transcendence, and by more or less the same means and practices of meditation and the elimination of the ego?" asked Kokkinophoros.

"These two traditions which may be called *sanaatana* and *shramana* respectively, do postulate transcendence of the worldly ego but they seem to talk differently about the final experience of transcendence. One talks of a positive joy, *rasa* and *ananda* and the other of cessation (*shama*) and nothingness (*shunyata*). One is joy(*rasa*) oriented, whereas the other is puritanical. The *sanaatana* contains eatables/ offerings (*havya*), tasting (*asvada*) and chewing (*carvana*) in the sacrifice (*yajna*), the other, that is the *shramana*, rejects sacrifice through fire but prescribes in its place the yogic practice, which may also be called the yogic fire, and the offerings in it are the breaths (*praana aahuti*) of the practitioner," added Pharatos.

Xenophon, who was feeling uncomfortable at this peroration could not help asking, "What I have never been able to understand is why you go on making a distinction between the *sanaatana* and the *shramana*, when the rituals of actual sacrifice or *yajna* has long ceased to be, except as a very rare practice, for nothing really dies in your homeland, Pharatos?"

"The distinction seems valid for a whole lot of reasons not just for the reason that the *sanaatana* stream hails from the sacrifices of the Vedic period," said Pharatos. "True, though yoga seems to have taken over very early as the most preferred method of achieving transcendence for both the *sanaatana* and the *shramana* traditions, not only the final state of *ananda* is positive and joyful but the attitude to life is also different. Whereas the *shramanas* have been arriving at *nirvana* through negation and rejection of all that life offers, the *sanaatanas* also posit a creator of the universe who comes to save and becomes a human incarnation (*avatara*) and plays out a life-cycle with a beginning, middle and end. The creator is missing in the *shramana* traditions, that is, among the Buddhists and the Jains. For them, there is the creation only."

"And hence the questions of how the creator looks after his own creation has not been paramount to the *shramanas*. It is only the individual cessation of suffering that has been their concern. Is that true?" asked Xenophon.

"They left many such questions to be answered by the *sanaatanas*. They also left matters of governance, aesthetics, state-craft, sexuality, erotica for the *sanaatanas* to wreck their brains on, except that many Jain ascetics have been fond of writing treatises on music and dance," added Pharatos. "The *shramanas* found great interest in architecture, temple building and paintings as these activities were necessary for their organizations. And they excelled in creating universities as they had a greater expertise in community organization."

"And therefore they borrowed more from the Mediterranean than others including their method of worshipping stone images of deities and their temples," said Kokkinophoros, "for they were more socially driven and valued the skills of community worship. It helped them to include others in their fold. The *sanaatana* tradition, it seems, was more geared to creating a sacred site of worship for a specified period to be vacated after the ritual session was over, such as a Vedic *yajna* or even a dramatic performance with its temporary wooden theater house. The *sanaatanas*, to begin with, were not so anxious to adopt temples, and that too made in stone, from the Mediterranean and Egyptian peoples. They adopted the Buddhist example much later. Don't you agree, Pharatos?"

"Yes, I do," said Pharatos. "Your perceptions of social actions and organizations are always valuable, as the commune system of life is your ideal and you have so much faith in the dictatorship of the guardians. But as the *shramanic* followers neglected the organization of civil governments, in the absence of militarily strong states the *shramanic* organizations were unable to protect themselves from loot and plunder and thus their followers dwindled in numbers. Their organizations (*sanghas*, *viharas* and *chaityas*), that once aided the expansion of their followers all over Asia, crumbled easily against the plundering forces of Islam. Strangely enough, the individualistic teacher and the practitioner of the *sanaatana* fold, proved to be better equipped to survive the onslaught of Islam, as the roving teacher, the mendicant *guru* and the creator of smaller sects based on a line of *gurus*. The *sanaatana* beliefs found a new lease of life in the practices of devotional worship or *bhakti* guided by solitary mendicants."

"Well, Pharatos, this is your analysis of the comparative resilience of the *sanaatana* and the *shramana* traditions under the adverse conditions prevailing after the advent of Islam in India. Of course, the issue needs to be probed very deeply as perhaps India is the only example of non-relinquishment of the native faith after such a long period of Islamic occupation. But other than the sociological reason that led to the downfall of *shramanas* and the individualistic survivability of the *sanaatanas*, is there a philosophical reason for the better resilience of *sanaatanas*? Is there any resilience present in the very nature of the search for *ananda* or unalloyed bliss that made the *sanatana* tradition survive and live and will perhaps deliver it now from the current attack of western Consumerism?" asked Socrates.

"The primary cause of its resilience is none other than the natural human yearning for bliss, which is not just a yearning for peace. It is so in the very nature of beings to seek a positive joy, as I said earlier, therefore *ananda* is also called *sahaj* and all of us search for that *sahaj*. The *bhakti* saints and poets rest their search in the proximity of their beloved deity and desire nothing else. For them that is transcendence or *ek-stasi* (ecstasy), like the song and dance of the Dionysians, another *ananda* tradition of sorts. The ancients of the Upanishads also sought after *ananda* and said that the *Brahma* is the true joy. "That is nothing else but joy", *raso vai sah*," concluded Pharatos.

"Merely because of joy, knowledge cannot be relegated to a secondary aim," said Socrates. "But I will not contradict you now, as it is time for our afternoon meal and the siesta." The company broke and left the platanos tree in isolation to wave in the breeze.

Index